How to Hire Great People

Tips, Tricks and Templates for Success

Dwight C. Douglas

DEDICATION

To the first person who hired me, and the last person who fired me.

Table of Contents

1.   A Brief Note Before We Begin

I wrote this book because I wanted to help employers like you find and hire great workers, but before we dig in I thought you might like to know a little bit about me.

I started working early in life with one major reason being I was in the right place at the right time. When one of the coveted newspaper delivery routes in my Pittsburgh, Pennsylvania hometown neighborhood became available I wanted that job, even though I was only ten years old. I met with the route manager and was asked to train with the current newspaper boy. He was about 16 years old and growing out of the job. While training with the kid, it became clear how difficult my new, daily work would be. Not only would I have to deliver 100 daily newspapers every weekday at 4PM, but also 32 early Sunday "bulldog" papers on Saturday night, plus I would need to get up at 5AM on Sunday to deliver 70 papers. Despite all this, I was totally up for the job and so enthusiastic I felt as if I was floating on air.

Back then, newspapers were bundled in lots of 50 with a thin steel wire keeping them together. The teenager who was training me decided to have some fun and began whipping me using some of the clipped wires. This was very painful, and I wasn't about to indulge his bullying. I told him that if he didn't stop I would tell the route manager and his parents. He snarled, "You do that punk, and I'll keep this route so you won't get it." I decided to do the right thing, even if it meant not getting the route, so I told on him. When both his and my parents learned of his threat to keep the route, my parents asked the boy if he really wanted to have this on his record. I guess he didn't because he quietly handed over the route in freezing temperatures on February 5, 1960. For the next eight years, I delivered newspapers on that route.

That newspaper job taught me so much. It's generally not a kid thing in America anymore, but back then making $12 a week was a giant step up from no allowance at all. In a sense, it was like running my own business because customers weren't billed. I went door-to-door to make collections. This early experience instantly disciplined me. When my route manager came around on Saturday, I had to pay the full amount. So, if I didn't collect all the money, the shortage had to come out of my pocket. The job also prepared me for future full-time jobs. In the job of newsboy, full time meant working every single day of the year.

I gave up the paper route as I approached college age, realizing it would be incompatible with my educational goals. To maintain an income, I signed up for the student worker program at Pittsburgh's Point Park University, and worked some interesting, but unusual jobs during my three years there. My first position was a weekend responsibility running the campus bowling alley. This meant checking people in and out, renting and restocking bowling shoes and manually setting the pins because there were no automated lanes back then.

Next, I became an elevator operator. My school had purchased an old, high-rise hotel with manual elevators requiring human attendants. Aside from having the frat boys dump a bucket of water on me, the ups and downs weren't too bad. After that, I became a painter's apprentice. Because the university converted the hotel into a dormitory for 400 students, all the rooms in that twenty-story building had to be painted.

Learning how to paint came in handy, saved me a lot of money throughout my life and it was one of my painting assignments that led to another work adventure. Point Park University owned the Pittsburgh Playhouse, and I was asked to paint some doors there. This led to a job offer to work in the box office, and I jumped at the chance of getting out of my painter's pants. It was not only fun being around the actors and actresses, but I was also learning about handling money and closing the books each night. I also did some ushering and because the theater ran movies in the summer, I saw *Yellow Submarine* over 300 times.

While working at the playhouse, I also did an on-air shift at my college radio station. Because I was paying my way through school, I had the opportunity to work some other summer jobs, one of which was a shipping clerk position at a bed factory. One day while working there, I painfully learned that you load the last stop into the truck first, not the other way around. I also worked one summer in a steel mill wearing metal-tipped shoes, and it was there that I got a good on-the-job education about what I didn't want to do for the rest of my life.

Having learned the ropes at my campus radio station lead to my first disc jockey (DJ) job at Pittsburgh's WAMO-FM, where I was paid a whopping $62 a week to do the 12 Midnight to 4AM shift while still trying to finish college. Being able to play whatever music I wanted made for enjoyable work, but after just a few months on the job the position was clearly taking a toll on my sleep and college life.

A Brief Note Before We Begin

Coincidentally, just as I was close to getting burned out, the radio station owners changed the format from Rock to Rhythm and Blues and all the white guys were laid off. That's the way radio often works.

That sudden unemployment led to my application for work at Pittsburgh's famous public TV station, WQED. One of the questions on the job application inquired why I had left my last job. I wrote, "racial situation." Ironically, I received a phone call about an hour after I dropped off my application and resume asking if I could come back for an interview. I walked into the office of the woman interviewing for the position and shook her hand. I was quite surprised when she asked, "You're Dwight Douglas from WAMO?" Almost immediately she wanted to know why I left that radio station. After I explained, she felt more comfortable with my provocative answer to the application question, and, because I was qualified, I got the job.

I became a telecine technician, working with film and photographic slides for WQED's *Newsroom* show and *Mister Rodgers Neighborhood*. And yes, I'm talking about the nationally syndicated TV show that starred Fred Rodgers. Working on that program was not only exciting but provided a wonderful opportunity to learn how television programs were created and produced. In addition, my work at the station brought about my first exposure to labor unions. After the workers unionized the shop, my salary went from $75 to $175 a week. I also saw firsthand the tensions, both imagined and real, between employees and management. Working at WQED also opened my eyes to the differences between nonprofit institutions and businesses.

After WQED, I took a job with a large national corporation, ABC — the American Broadcasting Companies. They owned and operated AM and FM radio stations in Pittsburgh and I started out as a part-time DJ on WDVE, the FM station. Later I became Production Manager at that station, then Program Director. It was the early seventies and my knowledge of rock music was greater than broadcasting experience, although I was acquiring those skills. The Program Director of a radio station is responsible for every single sound that is transmitted through the air, including the voices of the disc jockeys, so part of the job requires hiring, directing and firing the people who speak on the radio. In other words, it's a true management job. Being thrust into such a position at a relatively young age was challenging for me. Not knowing any better, I hired all my college radio friends to work at the station. I was naïve and far more interested in having fun than becoming rich. Despite my lack of experience and expertise, the station's ratings started rising and continued to grow through the years long after I left. Today, WDVE is often the number one rated station in Pittsburgh. I take pride in being one tiny germ that started the momentum.

Bouncing between three different radio stations in Pittsburgh was exciting and enjoyable but I was feeling a need to move on, so I left my hometown and landed a job at a new radio station named DC101 in Washington, D.C. After three years there, I moved to Atlanta, joining the country's largest radio broadcast consulting firm. During the next twenty-five years there I had the pleasure of working with over a hundred radio stations all around the world. Along with developing radio formats, I coached some of the industry's most famous radio morning shows. Howard Stern was just one of the personalities my firm helped with career advancement, leading him to a much bigger station, larger salary and, eventually, a platform where he became a household name. We helped many other broadcasters in the same way.

After twenty-five years spending much of my consulting time on the road, I wanted a change and took the Program Director job at an Atlanta radio station. Although I already knew about the hard work involved in managing the programming of a radio station and dealing with the pressure to maintain ratings, I learned that the work was something I preferred assisting others with rather than being directly in the thick of it. Eventually, I decided another change would be good so I left the station, moved to New York and joined an international software company that developed computer applications and systems for the radio industry. After sixteen years at that New York company, I retired and started to write books. You're holding one of them now.

As you can see, I've had a variety of job experiences as both worker and manager. I have done research on personnel for my clients, hired people myself and helped those hires move up in an industry where movement from one place to another means not only a new place to live but also greater prominence and more money. Along the way I learned much about marketing, in no small part by watching the way successful people propelled their careers through self-promotion. Radio is research driven, and this led to my acquiring skills in designing and deploying research studies and helping my clients implement programming changes to address the findings of the studies.

I'm being honest when I tell you that I have made some mistakes when hiring people, such as cleaning personnel who stole and a CFO who pilfered money in broad daylight. Mistakes are learning experiences, and when you learn from each mistake you make you become better at judging potential hires and helping your company reach and maintain success. There are ways to find great people, and I'll share some techniques with you in this book. There's also a need to keep the wonderful people you hire, so you won't get pulled away from your main job responsibilities to engage in a lengthy recruitment and interviewing process. I'll divulge some of my techniques in this regard as well.

I was always a little apprehensive when being interviewed for a job, so I have sympathy for anyone feeling nervous about going after a new position. I'm writing from the perspective of a manager, but you have also gone through the process of being recruited and hired. Perhaps you found your employer on your own, but are now in charge of hiring people and I hope you will enjoy and benefit from this book. I've kept it short and to the point so you can quickly dive into the process.

2.　Labor, Wages & Capital

There are vast differences between Karl Marx, Groucho Marx and Richard Marx. Karl Marx was an 1800s German philosopher, economist and historian. Julius Henry "Groucho" Marx was a 1900s comedian, writer, stage, film, radio and television star. Richard Marx is a pop and adult contemporary singer who has sold more than 30 million recordings, most of those when his career peaked in the 1980s.

We should all remember this quote from Karl Marx, *"Greek philosophy seems to have met with something with which a good tragedy is not supposed to meet, namely, a dull ending."* And, of course, who can forget Groucho's famous quote, *"One morning I shot an elephant in my pajamas. How he got into my pajamas I'll never know."* Here's a motivational lyric from Richard Marx' greatest hit, *"Wherever you go, whatever you do, I will be right here waiting for you."* Which always begged the question, if you love her so much why not stop waiting and go after her?

Let's throw the spotlight on Karl Marx for a minute. He and a guy named Friedrich Engels, who also had an unruly beard, wrote many words about the differences between communism and capitalism. Now before you get petrified because I used the word "communism," let me be perfectly clear. This book has nothing to do with that C-word but will focus on another C-word, capitalism. Marx and Engels were trying to figure out a fundamental business concept every manager deals with constantly. How much should you charge for your company's service or product and what is the best compensation to make sure your workers become and remain successful? A winning manager needs a grasp of these basics, so keep reading.

Karl Marx knew that capital was the force needed to create a business. Capital is money, and those having it were called *"capitalists."* The equations they employed to figure out how to make a product and sell it for a profit were key to every worker's income, even though the laborers were never given a look at precisely how those financial decisions were made. Said another way, the owner class didn't want the worker class to know the inner functioning of the business. This protected capitalists from being scorned and confronted about how their "living wages" were calculated.

To get the money needed to create corporations and businesses, mere mortals had to convince bankers to lend them cash, otherwise known as capital. Since these loans had to be paid back, a notion of selling shares of the business, or stock, provided the means to spread the risk over more than one person or bank. Remember the intent, as stated by Karl Marx, *"If we have chosen the position in life in which we can most of all work for mankind, no burdens can bow us down, because they are sacrifices for the benefit of all; then we shall experience no petty, limited, selfish joy, but our happiness will belong to millions, our deeds will live on quietly but perpetually at work, and over our ashes will be shed the hot tears of noble people."* As your writer has experienced, however, when the work of mankind isn't profitable the tears that are shed often happen in front of a sign that reads FACTORY CLOSED.

A symbiotic relationship exists between the two classes, worker and capitalist. If it's mutual, both parties benefit. There are other forms of capitalism such as commensalism, in which only one species benefits while the other is neither helped nor harmed. Then there's parasitism, where the bloodsucker gains while the host suffers. These last two are not typically found in healthy companies, but either can and do happen.

Bad management of pension funds, harsh union tactics or a complete failure of a corporation to control its worker class can drive an enterprise into the ground. A parasite might be a venture capitalist who buys a company, strips it of the very essence that made it successful, only to sell it later for a profit without the worker class benefiting at all. Parasitic vultures are everywhere.

When the workers of the world united two hundred years ago, many in the owner-capital class became fearful they would be forced to adopt a communal sharing of their wealth. Of course, that never happened. The gap between the wealthiest in the world and those who make less is still widening today, yet the source of this wealth gap, capitalism, has not stopped. Now maybe you just want to hire a new receptionist and don't want to solve the world's problems. I get that, but this background material will help you to understand the dynamics so please bear with me.

Let's consider some facts. People are necessary to create products and services and people manage people. From the first guy hired to shovel out a pig sty all those years ago to the advanced software programmer who will help propel today's billion-dollar idea, people are needed to do the work. There is a correlation between great people and great companies. Oh yeah, luck can certainly play a role but this book will help you rely less on chance and more on the techniques of hiring great people. It's an art to find them and a challenge to keep them, and as a manager you will be judged on the quality of the team you put together.

Collaboration is a key ingredient in an effective crew. It's the glue that holds a team together. No man is an island. Marx and Engels bounced ideas off each other's beards. Groucho's brothers motivated him to greatness. Richard Marx was inspired by his father, Dick Marx, a jazz pianist and musician who made money writing advertising jingles and soundtracks. Hey, a guy must eat.

We have become a nation of "jobbing it out," but this new norm doesn't always work or isn't always possible. Sooner or later, you will probably have to hire personnel. I worked for a software company whose people were located all around the world but working on the same project. Once a year they all got together to discuss the mission, lift some pints and break bread. This can work, but it takes a whole new way of thinking and doing. A partnership with another company can also be beneficial, although risky. It has the potential to produce massive breaches (think Edward Snowden) or major failures with dire consequences. People get killed when a business doesn't intelligently design and implement a jet plane's navigation system.

Companies and individuals are unique, and this book may have a few ideas about hiring and motivation that are not applicable to certain firms or people. Some of the most brilliant folks I have worked with over my sixty years in business have been horrible employees. I would add that some of them were crazy lunatics, but at the time they were the backbone of a successful franchise.

Business has a concept of expansion and contraction and this is the reason why seniority and time-on-the-job matters. As a manager, I have been forced to execute major cutbacks during lean times and suffered through sleepless nights with the heart wrenching task of deciding who will stay and who will go. It's another part of business reality.

In the quest to produce greater profit for their owners and stockholders, many companies have turned to offshore divisions where labor is cheaper. Their associative guilt might not be greatly felt because much of this migration occurred over a long period of time, but it has hurt workers deeply in certain countries. We are not going to cover the notion of "political economy" in this book, but it's worth mentioning that there are two highly debated forces: nationalism vs globalism.

Whether you are hiring developers at a software plant in India or parking lot attendants at your family restaurant in Indiana, the material in this book will help you. If you are job hunting, you will find a ton of good advice for you on these pages as well. It's not about tricking the system, but rather becoming more knowledgeable about the workings of business to increase your chances of getting hired. Additionally, you might climb the ladder of upward mobility and become a manager in the future, and the information conveyed in this book could greatly enhance your success.

It's one thing to keep bad seeds *out* of your business, but it's far more important to get the best people *into* your business. Once you have them, you need to hold onto them, and that involves far more than simply keeping them happy. Happiness is a vague notion and cannot be universally applied. You aren't a shrink; you are a manager. You must keep your focus while inspiring your team to keep theirs.

Hiring great people is the first step in making your labor force think beyond the notion of work as laborious. Work should be productive, motivational and *fun*. Wages will always be important but pay is not the sole requirement of worker contentment. So, let's dig into it now. Let's go find some great people!

3.   Tribes & Teams

Quite a few companies evaluate potential hires based on whether they will fit into the culture of the firm. Now this can get a little dicey because some social scientists and business gurus will tell you that if a company's employees become too like-minded the firm will suffer in the long run. In fact, diversity of opinion and expertise often sparks a major invention or marketing explosion.

When hiring, it's important to consider how a candidate is aligned with the shared values of your existing team. I was involved with what became a terrible situation in Detroit when I consulted my client to hire a new manager. The guy we hired was shunned immediately by almost everyone else who worked at the plant. After a tormenting quarter, my client asked me to find someone else. I wanted to find out what caused this manager's demise and, after relocating him to another job, I traveled back to Detroit to investigate. I was floored when talking with some of his former staff members over coffee. They explained that they hated his shoes and proudly chided, "No one in Detroit would wear those shoes." Really? I guess black motorcycle boots and clodhoppers were the rage at the time. I knew that deep down inside they disliked him for other reasons. We'll get to that later.

Speaking of footwear, people always ask what they should wear when going to a job interview and my plain-spoken answer is, it depends. If you are going for a shot as a welder at a mechanic shop you should not go black tie formal. On the other hand, if your interview is with a law firm, I suggest you wear a suit, tie and a good, well-polished pair of shoes. We judge people by many things and dressing appropriately for a job interview will enhance your chances of getting hired. When you are interviewing a potential hire, what they wear matters, to a point, so be observant and thoughtful in this regard.

At every turn during the interview process there are clues as to whether the man or woman sitting before you is going to be a terrific employee or an unmitigated mistake. I once interviewed a computer programmer/web site builder who was wearing casual slip on shoes and no socks. Later, my partner who participated with me in the interview said, "I don't think he will fit in. He didn't wear socks." I laughed and commented that, yes, we do judge people from head to toe, but I like his work. We hired him and he was fantastic. He was so incredibly talented that another firm lured him away within a year. Keeping great workers is a major goal, and we'll get into the details of how to do that later.

Some teams operate efficiently despite differences and conflicts within the group. Here's a baseball reference for you. Billy Martin managed some outrageously conflicted Yankee teams. The players squabbled amongst themselves, and Billy argued with the owner and the players. While all this was going on, the team won a boatload of games. There is a notion that chaos can breed achievement, but it can also generate resentment and turnover, which is generally not good in business.

In a work tribe, there is usually a trial for a new hire to establish themselves and gain the trust of their co-workers. Just like in the *"Mean Girls"* movies, a bit of "rookie challenge" might occur during a new employee's first weeks on the job. When the new guy gets playfully tricked by the veterans, it's a tribal test of his will to survive. As a boss, you should always watch carefully and wait before over-acting, but never endorse what is referred to legally as "hazing." If you don't know what that is, you should. It's any ritual that uses harassment, abuse or humiliation to initiate someone into a group, team or club.

The software company I worked for hired people from all over the world. We cast a wide net looking for the best software designers and programmers we could find. I remember the day a newly hired Chinese American woman walked into the cafeteria and sat down at a table where two others were eating an early lunch.

Once seated, two Taiwanese ladies welcomed the new employee to the company. The new designer's grandfather had immigrated to the United States sixty years ago and our new hire did not speak Chinese. Even after becoming aware that the newbie did not understand Mandarin or Cantonese, the two ladies continued to speak in their native tongue. I happened to observe this but decided not to get involved. Yes, it was rude behavior but sometimes you must choose your battles.

Things worked out quickly. The next day I saw the newly hired woman eating her lunch a little later, sitting at a table with three America-born workers like her. For the next ten years, she would sit at the same table with those co-workers. I did the right thing by not getting involved. The kids worked it out, just like they often do at daycare.

This brings up an important question about a company's culture. How much is created by the company itself compared to how much grows organically through the interactions of the workers? There is no absolute answer, but a culture always exists within a group of people. There are some experts who say that 250 people or more can lead to impersonal gang-rule. They talk of factions and cliques, which are the natural progression of any collective.

Through my more than fifty years of management experience, I have developed a theory about workers which I call the "third roommate syndrome." Think of an apartment situation with two tenants. Each of the roomies learns early on if they can get along. If it doesn't work out, one roommate moves on to a better situation. Things change when there are three roommates. Eventually, two of the roomies will turn against the third. So, why wouldn't this happen in a company, homeowners' association or a club? Well, it always has and always will.

People bond with like-minded souls. Who hasn't heard the expressions "work wife" and "work husband" to indicate the regular presence of a member of the opposite sex during work hours? Far from being unhealthy, these associations give people joy in the workplace by providing a trusted companion.

A manager must not overreact to any gossip in the plant. You cannot correct it, just be aware of it. Remember that the gatherings of people in the workplace bring about bonding and solid teamwork. Hopefully, they help propel the employees' and company's goals and projects. Some managers see cliques as disruptive and unproductive, but I would suggest such a person doesn't understand how people work.

There is more than drama that comes out of conflict. Sometimes great ideas emerge from struggles. When I worked in the radio business, it was natural for the sales department to view the programmers and disc jockeys with skepticism. Sales felt the talent had it easy and were overpaid. In software, there is a wall between web and graphic designers and those who write the software code. The designers believe coders have no sensitivity to appearance and esthetics while the coders believe the designers are a subset of human intelligence. Oh, the IT guys hate everyone. I joke, but these groupings of specific talents and experiences are a dynamic confluence which must be managed and directed to harmonious interaction.

Consider planning events, celebrations and other enjoyable gatherings of workers and management to bring people together and inspire good feelings about them and your company. One of my firms arranged an afternoon picnic and softball game, which was fantastic. Birthday parties, if inclusive, are another great way to offer a short work break to celebrate a co-worker and strengthen bonding among the team members. Other morale builders can be as simple as "Free Food Fridays" or "Causal Fridays."

As a manager, you must always consider the feelings of your employees. One of my companies had two divisions under one roof. At the monthly planning meetings of one of the divisions, a large lunch was brought in for the team. The other division never got food at their meetings. I remember one guy asking, "What are we? Chopped liver." I turned to him and smiled, "They had chopper liver, today?" This is just one example of how thoughtless practices can offend and hurt workers. Equality is a vital concept in business. How about free coffee? It's a relatively inexpensive way to show all employees you value them, and it helps them stay awake!

It's important to realize that people change, and over time workers can drift away from the tribe's culture. They no longer work as a team member and may become isolated with a desire to operate alone. Working from home, a new way of doing business in our digital world, can benefit those independent souls who prefer to hyper-focus on a task rather than being involved with team spirit. A skillful manager will constantly reevaluate collaboration, applying new arrangements as needed. There are many software services and programs on the market that make this kind of "groupthink" practical, shareable and beneficial.

Now here's a note for those who depend on outside headhunter firms to help with employee recruitment. An algorithm, a process or a set of rules to follow, can help you sieve through hundreds or even thousands of candidates, but the output is only as good as the input. Some of the recruitment sites do a fantastic job with a questionnaire for the manager that gives recruiters proper requirements and a profile for the opening, but they are simply mining data and they have no way to do any deep dive vetting. Ironically, people can fool the system by adding lies and misleading boasts to their application and most recruitment services do not verify the claims. This can mess up the pool of possible hires. Hey, people lie.

My advice is to be ultra-specific on a job definition and provide exact details on what you expect from the person who will be hired. If they must take the trash out, tell them that on the front end. If you are going to drug test them every month, be honest about it. If a security clearance is needed, explain that in clear language. One thing you shouldn't do is describe the specifics of the position down to what they must wear or what they should eat. When I worked in India, no one wore shoes. If you look too much like a cult, you could scare talented people away.

There is a great word to describe the primary goal of any tribe or team, **camaraderie**. It simply means mutual **trust** and **friendship** among people who spend a lot of time working together, and those are two key ingredients in a well-managed business.

It's important to build strong teams and you must be flexible to accept the reasonable needs and requests of the tribe. Beyond all the rules and regulations, your footprints will become the things employees say about your company. If they declare, "It's a great place to work," then you are probably doing many things right. The opposite response travels fast, and as one former employee said to a job hunter, "Steer clear of those guys." You don't want that kind of aura surrounding your company.

4.   Rules & Regulations

We've come a long way from the time when only men had jobs and women stayed at home with the kids. As the workplace evolved, a need to establish rules and regulations came about.

History shows most of the major office changes in the early part of the twentieth century were pushed through by labor unions on a quest to keep their workers safe. They also negotiated and gained higher wages for the rank and file.

Abuse of women in the workplace has been a long-standing problem, and the federal government established rules outlining what may and may not be discussed during an employment interview. Here are some questions you must never ask. "Do you have any children? If so, how many and what are their ages? Are you single, married, divorced, or engaged? What kind of childcare arrangements do you have in place? Are you currently taking any form of birth control or fertility treatment? What are your plans if you get pregnant? Does your spouse work? If so, how do they make their living? Should we refer to you as Mr., Miss, or Mrs.?"

Common sense would suggest most of those questions are a severe invasion of privacy, but some interviewers, perhaps wanting to seem friendly and causal, may drift into those waters without understanding the implications. To judge a candidate based on their family structure is not only wrong, it's illegal. Marital status might be a question a guy would ask a woman at a bar, but the question must never be asked during a job interview or in the workplace. Some people

21

may list their date of birth on their resume, but you shouldn't ask their age.

You might assume that if they don't offer personal information, they simply don't want to tell you. I've had employees who worked with me for years surprise me with the introduction of their spouse at a holiday party.

The birth control question not only violates a woman's right to privacy, but if asked after they are employed is a violation of the Health Insurance Portability and Accountability Act (HIPAA). It's clear and states an employee's health records are not to be disclosed to anyone.

These questions are **acceptable** under the law and you should ask them. "Do you have any restrictions preventing you from traveling? Do you have any conflicting commitments that would affect your work schedule? Do you anticipate any recurring or lengthy absences from work?" These questions are grounded in reasonable and legal language and cover important need-to-know aspects of an applicant's life.

If you are interviewing a person for a comptroller position requiring travel to company branches, they would not be a viable candidate if they are on the do-not-fly list. There was a time I hired a person and forgot to ask if they had any commitments that would conflict with their work schedule. The first day of his employment, my new hire walked in and said that he was going away for the next two weeks to attend an out of the country wedding he was invited to a year before. Now, I could have been a jerk and disallowed the time off, but

I had just hired him and knew he would be great on the job. I calmly reminded him that no one gets vacation time until they have been employed for six months or more, and I adjusted his start date to solve the problem. Just be sure to check with your Human Resources (HR) lawyer before you do something like this.

I also had an employee who left work two hours early every Wednesday to help Meals on Wheels distribute lunches to shut ins. She always worked additional hours to offset her time away and I honored her requests but I wished I had asked about her commitments during the interviewing process.

This may be a good place to share an important caveat. Not everyone is a good interviewer. Some managers think an interview is a good time to do their comedy routine or to pitch the greatness of the company. The presentations of some interviewers are so bombastic the interviewee feels that getting the job would be the worst possible outcome because trying to express themselves would be difficult.

Believe it or not I have seen people interview prospective employees by airing out the company's dirty laundry. I can't fathom their motivation, other than a desire to save some innocent person from the depression of working there. No workplace is perfect, but you should never discuss whatever negativity you may feel about your company when interviewing a prospective hire.

You should never ask a candidate if they have worked at a union shop or inquire about their feelings toward labor unions. It could come back to bite your company if the Labor Relations Board is ever called in to mediate a problem. However, if the position your candidate is interviewing for at your company falls under the collective bargaining agreement of a labor union, you must disclose that to them. In a lawsuit brought in the early 1970s, by the conservative commentator William F. Buckley, it was decided that no one can be forced to join a union, but they still must pay the dues. Perhaps you let your HR department handle this transaction in which local laws might apply.

You certainly don't want to be the fool who asks what holidays a candidate observes. That can be construed as a trick question to uncover their religion, an aspect of their life which should never be discussed during an interview or in the workplace.

You also cannot ask about political affiliations. That is none of the company's business and a good manager will never ask such questions. Focus on your applicant's skills, experience and work history, rather than going off script into personal territory.

Speaking of scripts, before going into an interview with a potential employee, an accomplished executive will have prepared a list of questions with plenty of white space to take detailed notes as the candidate answers them. I will outline some of my techniques for interviews in the next chapter, but here's the headline. Be prepared. If you ask each interviewee the same questions and document their answers, you will be able to compare and evaluate their responses once all your interviews are complete.

Here's something that doesn't occur as frequently as it should, a comprehensive examination that tests an applicant on their knowledge about the established procedures of the industry, common rules, laws and techniques that must be known before the person begins their employment. I worked in the software business as a marketing guy, not a developer. I interfaced with many teams as the marketing VP and, for some reason, I was sent on a software coder recruitment trip to Northeastern University in Boston. They have a fantastic apprentice program called "Cooperative Education," where master's degree candidates leave the university for six months to work in their desired field. Companies, especially hi-tech firms, love this arrangement, although it can be costly for a business.

Why would they send me? Well, I was skilled at finding good people, not necessarily the best programmers. There is a difference between how a person presents themselves and their job skills. I am sure Mozart would have been a terrible interviewee. Elton John wasn't such a brilliant candidate for music school, although he was immensely talented. Testing came into play on this mission. We had a PhD at the firm who developed a highly effective test for computer programmers, that allowed him to ascertain the technical chops of each applicant. It was more important they knew their way around code than whether they laughed at my jokes, but my involvement with interviewing allowed my firm to evaluate candidates on two levels. Was the potential employee a good person as well as skilled in the technical aspects of the job? You can teach a great person new skill, but a jerk will never change. Your company will be better off by not even considering such a person.

At the beginning of this chapter, I talked about women in the workplace and how their arrival changed our governance in companies, all for the good. Men can be pigs, as we have seen with the seemingly endless list of males being outed for their wretched habits of sexual harassment in the workplace. This is serious business.

Each complaint against a man brought in a woman's "wrongful termination" lawsuit, which is a legal term, could cost his company between 100 and 200 thousand dollars. If the problem is systemic, that amount could blast into the millions. So, what exactly is sexual harassment and how come some men and women don't understand the law? Let's make it simple and clear.

The United States' Equal Employment Opportunity Commission (EEOC) defines workplace sexual harassment as *"unwelcome sexual advances, requests for sexual favors, and other verbal or physical conduct of a sexual nature."* Some experts report that 51% of people have said they've been hassled by a supervisor while 49% complained about non-management co-workers, so this is not solely a boss problem.

Whatever the source, harassment within an enterprise can deeply affect the company and place it at legal risk. It's an important part of your job to make sure it isn't happening in your workplace.

One aspect of on-the-job harassment is hostile working conditions. An environment created by a boss or co-worker whose actions, communication or behavior make it extremely difficult or impossible for another to do their work is a major problem. This kind of bad behavior alters the terms, conditions, and reasonable expectations of a comfortable work setting for employees.

I am not trying to be funny, but a job environment is often a breeding ground for romantic relationships. I'm sure some of your friends met their spouse or significant other on the job. There is nothing wrong with this, and if you found the love of your life in the workplace then more power to you. Just remember there are implications which should be taken seriously. We'll cover them shortly.

Let's get back to harassment, which is already in progress. We all are drawn to attractive people. Some managers will hire one person over another because of their appearance. I remember the time when an attractive lady was sitting in the lobby before her job interview with me. Many of the guys walked by my office to give me a thumbs-up on the possible hire. Disgusting, yes, but that's exactly the way some men are wired. Be careful when hiring or taking any action in the workplace. Carefully consider the legal definition, "Unwelcome Sexual Advances, requests for sexual favors and other verbal or physical conduct of a sexual nature." A job interview can lead to a lasting relationship with a new hire, so begin it properly. Shake their hand, when we get back to that custom, and ask them to be seated. At this moment, you are an ambassador for the company and their first impression of you can color the way the interviewee will forever see your company.

Always remember that things such as touching a woman or man, looking down a woman's blouse, making sexual jokes or remarks or calling a female applicant "doll," "honey" or "baby," are against the law. Should you think it's cool to drift into a titillating description of last year's holiday party, then you have a problem.

Whether you agree or not, things like back massages, touching another's hair, rubbing yourself, brushing up against someone else, or making "elevator eyes" by checking out a person from head to toe are all wrong. Actions like those create a hostile, sexually charged work environment. Remember, it's not about your intent but rather the way your actions or comments are interpreted by your employee, or applicant.

Recently, several high-profile men have been taken down with the #MeToo movement. They either didn't know the rules or decided that they were so powerful those laws didn't apply to them. You need to learn the lessons of losers like them, otherwise you could be repeating them, causing your company to spend on legal actions, and destroying faith in a fair system of American employment. You could also end up in jail.

Rules and regulations do change, and most large companies make employees take tests and attend seminars about the shifting regulations in the workplace. Solid governance is good business. The rules help people understand the difference between real life and corporate responsibilities.

Yes, you might be dating someone in your workplace, but keep in mind your company could ask one of you to leave. There are many companies that have "no dating" policies, but before you write one at your firm consult a labor lawyer. Some states protect workers' privacy and if one dating person doesn't supervise the other, a state law may not permit such a draconian rule.

The person who is engaged in a romantic relationship in the workplace will have to decide if that makes sense for them. Another possible price for a love liaison at work could be your company moving your significant other far away from your day to day decision making processes. There are also dangerous and destructive cases in which a manager with the power to hire and fire exerts pressure on someone into a romantic relationship or demands sexual favors. This might be hard to prove in a court of law, but emails and text messages could be a deadly trail of truth. That is not the kind of boss you want to be.

By the way, a person having influence over another who hires or fires doesn't have to necessarily be a manager. For example, if an employee has a vote in a committee and they disclose they will "put in a good word for you," then they are on very thin ice. You certainly don't want to write that in an email. These are the things that employment lawyers look at when they litigate for damages.

If you are in business and you haven't watched at least a few episodes of the TV show *Mad Men*, you should. In the 1950s and 1960s, women who climbed to power often did so from the position of receptionist or secretary, and in some cases on their knees. I'm not being rude but simply stating a fact that the "good old boy" network kept a lot of people down, especially women.

We are well beyond the mentality of those long-gone days, but we haven't fully escaped the dark past. People are judged on appearance and personality and, sadly, statistics show attractive people get more promotions and higher pay increases. Avoid rewards based on non-work attributes. Hire and reward smart and effective people.

Be sure to understand a candidate before you hire them but do so without invading their privacy. Their talent or potential shouldn't be masked by laws, regulations and rules. If they have the desire and aptitude to learn and advance, give them a chance to show you who they really are. Give the employee the chance to talk during your first encounter and listen to what they say. You aren't hiring yourself; you are hiring another. Shut up and listen carefully.

5. Headhunters & Social Media

The internet is a crazy place. I grew up before the online world became a thing and was deep into my career as it started soaring to the position of power and influence it holds today. Many of us "old timers" found ourselves straddling a giant crevasse splitting the earth. We had to decide whether to jump into the future or stay on the other side with our pencils, papers and analog realities.

The business world changed with the introduction of the IBM Personal Computer in 1981, and many companies began computerizing their workflows. Although the internet was conceived by the US Government in the 1960s, it didn't become a reality until the 1980s when a good number of military and educational institutions became electronically linked. The expansion of the internet into the corporate world took place in the 1990s, causing a profound change in commerce that continues today. Not only did the internet become a tool for legacy companies, it turned out to be a business unto itself for the many tech startups of that era. The lawless part of the internet has never been tamed. Just look at the problems that Twitter and Facebook have concerning privacy.

Thirty years ago, I said the internet had two great purposes, learning things and buying things. The humans behind the internet curtain were either showing or selling.

Working in the software business gave me insight about how the internet's progression has dramatically changed the world. Because the internet has no borders, a vast worldwide resource became available. When you wanted to hire the best computer programmers, instead of advertising in the local paper, you casted your net to billions worldwide. This is one reason why the internet became known as the World Wide Web, which is the genesis of the "www" portion of many website addresses.

As I adjusted to the fact that an applicant might be 10,000 miles away, I turned to other technologies like Face Time and Skype to arrange personal interviews. I looked at each candidate's social media accounts to determine if they might be a good fit for my company. Mining a person's Facebook or Twitter posts is the modern-day equivalent of an expensive background check by a private investigator or a corporate drug test. Yes, the poison found on a person's social media platform can help you avoid hiring an individual you would never want in your company. Good corporate governance requires you to find and analyze those public comments and pictures, and you should feel free to confront any potential hire if you see something questionable.

From its very beginning, LinkedIn focused on the business world. Even though they force feed some stupid social media behavior to their members, they are still a valuable resource for finding and gaining knowledge about people worth hiring. If you are looking for a job, you should be on LinkedIn. If you are hiring, then use their search tools to find candidates. This brings me to a fundamental truth. Some of the best people aren't looking for a job; you must lure them away from the one they already have. We'll get into this concept more deeply a bit later.

I've successfully used headhunters over the years to find some wonderful workers. In the old days of software recruitment, we used what were then called "body shops" to locate young coders from India and other Asian countries. These offshore recruitment firms moved a dozen or so young programmers to America, put them up in houses and then placed them as temporary workers in various companies in "try before you buy" situations. If a temp was good and the company wanted to keep him or her, they would start the H1B visa application process. My company retained a law firm solely dedicated to this task. While you might argue that importing workers is bad from a nationalistic viewpoint, greed did open the doors to globalization. It's a new reality that is not the result of a business strategy, but an authentic desire to hire the best.

Headhunters typically found great people but working with them was expensive. Some firms charged as much as $20,000 for the first and second years of the placement. This meant the worker would not be getting a raise for that period. When unemployment percentages go down, the market for good people accelerates and the demand increases the price of recruitment. The internet can become somewhat of an equalizer when a potential hire sees your opening and applies directly.

I'm sure some job hunters have been taken advantage of by nefarious actors or recruitment companies, charging a considerable fee with a bogus guarantee of placement. Only later does the person looking for work find out they were deceived, much like a student ensnared with a phony university promising them a degree and delivering nothing.

Some of the recruitment web sites provide a dashboard for employers to detail desires and needs, but the only true way to know what a given candidate has to offer is a face-to-face meeting. When I worked in radio, it was easy to locate talented people. In that business, each disc jockey looking for work has a recording of their on-air act, called an aircheck, which they submit for evaluation to those stations where they want to work. Here's a true story. When I was trying to convince the General Manager of a station in Washington, D.C. to hire Howard Stern, the guy agreed without meeting Howard or even listening to his aircheck. That situation turned out extremely well, but there was a potential for a lunatic who could have destroyed the radio station.

Be careful with social media and internet postings. Things you read there could be lies. It amazes me how many people have gotten prestigious jobs, only to later admit they never attended the university on their resume. I am always careful to say I attended college, but never made it seem like I graduated, which I did not. I have no regrets about prematurely ending my college education. I wanted to get out and start working to make money. Lying about my college background never crossed my mind, but I'm sure there are others who do so. Some even lie about military service, for whatever reason. So, my advice to you when hiring is to always dig deep and find out what's real. No company wants a liar on their team.

Recently, some politicians have been embarrassed by what the press found in their high school and college yearbooks. I wrote the captions for the pictures in my high school yearbook and must say I am mortified about how unfunny some of my comments were, but I never dressed in blackface. Yes, it's possible to go back and see what someone's yearbook shows but judge it in context. We all made mistakes when we were young. In my case, I was the guy who decided what to publish, not my fellow students. I sure hope I didn't ruin anyone's career!

I constantly write, and some of my words have brought trouble. Once I authored an article titled, "The Death of Classic Rock," only to have to answer why I used those words when I applied for a job at a Classic Rock radio station. Today, it's still uncomfortable when someone brings up that piece. There are internet service companies who can find and scrub clean your mentions on the web, but good luck with that. The internet and computers are two things that seem to hold and disclose secrets more than people who work in the White House.

When interviewing, be careful asking about the candidate's social media posts, lest you come off as big brother or creepy spy. It is far too easy to fall into the trap of asking about a photo or post in a way that breaks one of the rules and regulations we already covered. See the Facebook picture of a woman applicant with a guy and ask, "Is that your boyfriend?" Oops!

If you feel compelled to ask about something seen on a candidate's internet post, you might be wasting your time even talking with the person. Judgement is needed, but if an off-the-rails rant makes you cringe, you could very well be seeing a weakness in reasoning on the applicant's part. College students are notorious for posting stupid pictures of drinking games or a dorm room shot where there are 99 bottles of beer on the wall. Before one of my kids applied for law school, she made sure all her embarrassing or questionable photos were gone. Some people turn off or delete their social media accounts when applying for work. After getting the job they turn them back on, and then the employer asks the HR department, "How did we miss this?"

You might want to ask an applicant how often they use social media and approach it this way, "Hey, is there anything on your social media platforms that you are embarrassed about?" That at least starts the conversation about how your company views social media and, more than anything else, the candidate's reaction can be a window into their mind or soul. Additionally, the query gives you an opening to explain your firm's policy about its expectations of how workers should use social media. You also must make a distinction between an employee's personal use of social media and any marketing policies you might have in place for them to advance your brand. Once an employee comes onboard with your company you need to monitor and manage what they post.

My company had an overseas office that decided to create their own public Facebook page. They wanted to use it to bond the team and to recruit hires. You know, "Look at this great place to work at and see our fun parties and celebrations." That was fine until one Friday afternoon when I saw Facebook conversations between the employees there that trashed the company and that office. Remember, this was a public account. We went into battle mode, deleted the posts, and asked the local manager if he had a problem with the staff. Our investigation found definite issues at the unit. In this case, social media led us to a problem but it would have been better had the local employees felt more comfortable picking up the phone and telling someone at the home office. Public whistleblowing is bad for business.

Social media is here to stay but we all must use it wisely. Now I'm about to make a statement which might sound a bit old fashioned, but I become concerned when an applicant posts too many messages. If someone created 11,000 Twitter messages in three years, how did they get anything else done? Some become obsessive with the internet, and I suppose that's part of its charm. What other product, outside of addictive drugs, has the kind of power to make us consistently check for feedback? It's why courts and Congress have rules in place for certain meetings or hearings where phones must be left outside the meeting room or turned off.

Should we ask how much time a person spends with social media before we hire them? I say yes because their answer can reveal personal priorities. All other things being equal, if one candidate uses social media a couple of hours every day and another jogs for two hours daily, the right hire is likely the latter, if for no other reason than the former might carry their obsession into every workday. Investigating personal lives can get a little tricky and you must never cross a line with certain questions, but it's in your company's best interest to know exactly how personal cell phone and internet use might affect an employee's productivity while on the job.

I remember when local governments started to ban smoking in the workplace. At offices in large buildings, people would gather their smokes and often find fellow smokers to go with them. Then it's an elevator ride to the ground floor, a walk to the building exit, smoking and talking outside, and finally a walk back to the elevator which returns them to their job. I decided to clock the process and found that people who take frequent smoke breaks spent about 40 hours a year away from their job. Wow, those smokers got an extra week off! Social media is less harmful than cigarettes, but you get the idea.

If you are working or job hunting, it's time to get wise about the need for internet discretion. If you are the kind of person who posts stupid things on the internet when drunk or on a power trip, you could get fired. Ask Rosanne Barr. For those people who didn't get a job because they failed to see the damage their social media profile created for them; change things up now. Examine all your public posts, just as your manager or future employer would do. Delete all mean and immature comments and get serious about landing a great future. Facebook didn't pay you to post those irresponsible remarks, and your future employer will not pay you to waste time online. Go for the money.

6.   Tricks & Temperaments

I confess to my use of unusual, but never unethical, ways of learning about the quality of a job applicant. Once, when considering a candidate for a position at one of my client's radio station, I was told that he was prone to corruption and bribery. I scheduled the interview in my hotel suite, positioning the guy on the sofa while I sat on a chair across from him. Before he got to the room, I placed a butterscotch candy, a peppermint candy and a stick of gum on the coffee table between us. I said nothing about my staging and did not offer him anything as we started talking causally. During the interview, without the slightest hesitation, he reached down and picked up the striped peppermint candy, unwrapped it and put it in his mouth. I wasn't doing a consumer survey on what flavor he liked best; I was trying to figure out who this person truly was.

When I reported back to the client who wanted my advice on the various applicants I interviewed, I advised the company to not hire the peppermint candy guy, even though it was the manager's personal pick for the position. I said, "David, I don't think he can be trusted." He reacted defensively and demanded that I explain myself. After I told him what I had done, he laughed and said, "What are you talking about? You were in a hotel room. Anyone would do that!" After I explained I had done the same thing with all the candidates, he asked a great question, "Well, did anyone else take the bait?" I replied there was only one, a young lady who obviously was nervous and suffering from the curse of dry mouth. She politely asked if she could have a candy.

This story has a strange ending. First, the manager proceeded to hire the peppermint guy. Then, because he thought I would have trouble working with the recruit, he fired me from my consulting role. I knew that the manager had his own agenda and I really didn't want to argue or become emotional. After all, it was just business. Now don't take a stand on this just yet. There's more to the story. About six months later I got a call from a friend who worked and lived in my former client's city. He opened with, "Hey, have you heard about that guy you call peppermint boy? They fired him. He did something illegal." I sat back in my chair and thought about all the times when one of my hires ended up being suspicious, secretive or deceptive and I just couldn't see any early warning signs. You'll never be able to fully investigate the soul of someone you're interested in hiring, but always keep your eyes open for any subtle warning signs and be even more vigilant should you receive any negative information on a candidate. Even the best shrinks are sometimes fooled by sick actors. You will never achieve perfection but always aim for the highest possible score.

If you think my observational method was unfair, well, I learned the trick from Thomas Edison. When the great inventor interviewed candidates for research positions, he would offer them a bowl of soup. He wanted to see if they would add salt or pepper to the soup before they tasted it. He figured that someone who would assume the soup needed to be seasoned without first evaluating the evidence right before them would not make a good research assistant. Every time I put salt on my food before tasting, I think of Thomas Edison and light bulbs. Okay, I'm the crazy one.

The quality of a potential hire's work and their prior experience should always be the primary driving factors in your hiring process, but these things aren't always apparent or maybe a candidate's past work doesn't exactly mesh with the requirements and goals of your project or product. Radio talent is an unusual breed of folk. Their skill at performing and entertaining an unseen audience often comes at the cost of some major or minor personality disorders. I had a good friend who aimed at putting together a workplace that was peaceful and cooperative, rather than being driven by egomaniacal super stars. That can work, but most of the time the quality of someone's work is affected by their personality. A prima donna of the stage can be highly disruptive in a normal workplace.

I have always drawn a circle and, at equal distances on that circle, I write the four temperaments of people. This isn't something I cooked up on my own. It goes back to the Greek physician Hippocrates, yes, the oath guy who described the four temperaments as part of his ancient medical concept about human personality traits and behaviors. Of course, I modernized them and applied the concepts to my potential hires and employees. Have a look.

The four traits are, 1. Creative-Artistic, 2. Negative-Judgmental, 3. Social-Sales and 4. Crazy-Outrageous. In any business, project or community gathering, you will see each of these four temperaments reflected in the associated people who rear their beautiful, and sometimes ugly heads. Let's take a closer look.

Some of my favorite people are Creative-Artist types. We look in awe at what they do with their eyes, hands and brains. One of the things that most people say about Apple's late, great leader, Steve Jobs, is that he wasn't a computer programmer; he was a marketing genius. The basis of his success was rooted in the fact that he was a Creative-Artistic person. The products had to look a certain way and his demands for style were more artistically centered than technological or sales oriented. Creative people can sometimes be brooding and overly emotional on certain aspects of business, but their charm and eye are needed to differentiate their company's products from those of all competing firms. Always involve Creative-Artistic folk with imaginative endeavors like logos, letterhead, advertising and imaging. Their touch can leave a lasting impression

Next, the Negative-Judgmental person can be a huge pain in the ass. We hate when they walk into a meeting, but deep down inside we know we need them to help us make informed decisions. If you don't have one on your staff, the team tends to do what the leader wants without any consideration of the various ways things that can go wrong. The Negative-Judgmental is the person who asks a good question that needs an answer, especially when it points out a major flaw in your idea. They aren't trying to make you look bad. If they are a good judge of negativity, they might just lead you to something wonderful you didn't even consider.

A company that doesn't employ a certain number of Social-Sales types will never be successful. Keep in mind this is coming from someone who fought long and hard with salespeople all along my career path. Someone must present an idea, product or service to someone else, and when they are highly skilled they become a major asset to their firm. Being optimistic is a good thing, and successful selling is the mark of one whose priorities are aimed at the success of their product or service. When they successfully sell, money flows into the business as well as their own pockets.

Then there are the daredevils and "outside-of-the-box" people, the Crazy-Outrageous temperament types. Ted Turner had two nicknames, one was "The Mouth of the South" and the other was "Captain Outrageous." The latter was his key to business success. Ted admitted he suffered great mental stress, but he never let his personal demons get in the way of a totally outrageous but viable idea. Sure, he got in trouble and embarrassed himself more than a few times, but in the end Ted Turner became the poster boy for the Crazy-Outrageous temperament. These types of people bring sparks and edginess into a business, which can often become the launchpad of success. Make no mistake, workers in this group will probably be your most difficult challenge as a manager, but you need their energy, quirky ways and ideas in your framework.

Now I offer a short lesson about how to use this information. People don't necessarily fit into just one category. I have seen a perfectly grounded Social-Sales type flip into an agile Negative-Judgmental when they thought something wasn't going to work. I have also seen the metamorphosis of a Creative-Artistic type when they leapt into a Social-Sales mode wanting to promote their ideas. Let's not be Negative-Judgmental about those who point out the bad aspects of an idea. That's a creative pursuit in and of itself.

You wonder who a person is before you hire them. Even using tricks, administering tests and asking good, hard questions won't reveal how a new hire might change when placed on a team that has been together for a long time. Yes, people can adjust their temperament to fill a void in a team. There's nothing wrong with this, but understand that a great salesperson will probably never sit down with Photoshop to create graphics for an advertising campaign. They will be able to distill and explain the major sales propositions and marketing points but let an artist choose the words and create the eye candy of the advertising.

Sometimes people display more than one temperament. I have seen crazy-outrageous people rein in their outlandishness to operate within sound business principals when they must. Ted Turner became a bison rancher and made tons of money doing it. Not only that, he could sell anyone on why that was a great idea for the bison, for the environment and for his bank account.

Your role as a manager is not to placate each of these temperaments, but to massage them, manage them and lead them to doing their best. You might not want to bring a Negative-Judgmental into an early brainstorming session. No one likes a "Debbie Downer" when you are trying to kickstart ideas. However, the meeting to prioritize the final list of ideas might be the perfect time to invite that challenger into the room. I once attended a conference where a preposterous software development plan was presented and I replied by saying, "Let's put together a sober timeline." I wasn't trying to be negative, but the use of the word "sober" instantly changed the dynamic in the room. All the experienced people knew the suggested plan was impossible, but now we had to commit to the reality of a solid estimate of the time needed to complete the project. The original suggestion of six months became at least one year when looked at soberly. The actual timeline became two years to craft a product with only basic features and none of the astounding bells and whistles initially planned for six months of work. For any worthwhile endeavor you're probably going to need at least two years, the same amount of time it typically takes to make a movie.

Customize these ideas for your business. All these observations continually erupt in any group dynamic. The hires and operations of a school board are much different than those of a fast-food franchise, but there are common basics between them. People are human beings. They take on different roles and their value is not a constant given. A person should be understood before they are hired, reevaluated after they join and continuously monitored as they progress through your company. People are more than negative, or social, or crazy or creative; they are the sum of all their experiences and friends, and always remember that friends work harder for friends.

I personally don't like to take tests, but there are times they help you get at the truth. More on a test I created, in the next chapter.

7.   The Douglas Test

There are a good number of professionally recognized tests that successful businesses use to help determine who you should hire. You may recognize names like the Caliper Profile, the Myers-Briggs Type Indicator, the SHL Occupational Personality Questionnaire, the Hogan Personality Inventory (HPI) and the DiSC Behavior Inventory. These instruments are highly valuable means of helping a recruiter or interviewer shape opinions about potential employees, but tests like Myers-Briggs can also be used to evaluate the management potential of current employees.

I worked in the cable television, radio broadcasting, software development and writing industries where things are a bit different, because the job hires in those businesses are based on previous work or a very convincing verbal pitch. As my experience grew, I wanted to find a better way to evaluate the personalities of the people I was considering.

I became inspired when I was interested in a job applicant. It was 1987 and my budget was miniscule. I had limited resources to recruit a new consultant for my firm, but I needed to figure out this applicant's temperament regarding the importance of money. I created eight index cards and asked my candidate to place them in order of importance to him.

Here are the eight cards:

1. To be needed, 2. To be known, 3. To be respected, 4. To be liked, 5. To be admired, 6. To be loved, 7. To be wealthy and 8. To be stroked (flattered).

The Douglas Test

to be needed

to be known

to be respected

to be liked

to be admired

to be loved

to be wealthy

to be stroked
(flattered)

This story had a happy ending for my prospective hire. After a good talk about what he wanted to do with his career and why he wanted to join our firm, he picked up the cards.

He ordered the cards on the desk in front of him, placing the "to be wealthy" card far down in his layout. I offered him the job and he accepted what I had considered a small starting salary. I was now armed with the knowledge that he was more interested in the work than the money, knowing there was a potential for raises down the road. He stayed with the company for more than fifteen years and was amply rewarded for his loyalty and hard work over that time.

My little card game became an obsession. I enticed many friends and co-workers into the role of guinea pigs as I used these cards to learn more about the people I was working with and interviewing. I even had one of my radio-psychologist friends do a research project with 2,000 people in the broadcasting industry. He analyzed the job types in radio against the Douglas Test and verified that people who elevated certain cards had a better aptitude for certain positions inside a radio station.

There is certain logical sense when analyzing the results of a Douglas Test layout. For example, when interviewing for a sales position, you would want the applicant to place the "to be wealthy" card in one of the first three positions. A keen desire to make money is an important ingredient in the personality profile of a highly social-sales type.

When recruiting for the broadcasting business, if an applicant placed the "to be stroked (flattered)" or the "to be known" cards in one of the top three positions, I worried that the person's priorities would conflict with some basic teamwork principles. If a person's driving force is "to be known," they might not work well with others. Their desire for publicity could get in the way of what's best for the entire team. Giving credit to those who do good work is an important aspect of management and a great motivational power. The term "stroked" is old-fashioned now, which is why I added the word "flattered" to the card. I also learned something interesting when the Douglas Test was translated into French. Workers in France who took the test were not impressed. The concept of flattery was insulting to them.

Think about this for a second. If a potential hire said one of their top three important desires was to be stroked and flattered, their boss and company could be dealing with a lot of their personal baggage on the job. I have heard the phrase "star baby" used for people whose egos must be constantly reinforced. Seeing that card high on a person's list might indicate that you are interviewing a narcissist.

Over the years I discovered that there was a vast difference between "to be admired" and "to be respected." Many times, an older person placed "admired" in a top position, as in "admired" by an industry or those who work for them. The "respected" card indicates a strong person who is merely asking to be treated fairly in the workplace and in life. I've noticed women often put this card in one of the three top positions. Both "respected" and "admired" are strong indications of management potential.

When the deep thought indicator cards, "to be liked," "to be loved" and "to be needed" get placed into one of the top three positions, we must carefully probe the person to understand their meaning. I remember asking the vice president of a company to take the Douglas Test. He arranged the cards in his preferred order, and I was curious about why he put "to be needed" in the second slot. He said, "Well, I always want to be able to be the guy who is needed. You know, the person who gets things done."

About two years later, after he was promoted to president, we had dinner. Over drinks, I asked him if he remembered the cards. He smiled and replied affirmatively. I pulled them out of my pocket and asked him to arrange them again. He quickly positioned the cards and I was surprised to see that "to be needed" was next to last. I pointed out to him that the first time he ordered the cards "to be needed" was second on his list. He quickly answered, "That was when I was the VP. Now I'm the president. Of course, I'm needed!"

This was the very first time I thought about what I comically came to refer to as "title-I-tis," a disorder in some people who need the confirmation that comes with a title. Some people see their value in the workplace based on the job position printed on their business card. I get that, but what if you are hiring someone who will never get a business card or title?

Then there's the little nugget, "to be liked," which can tell you a lot about a person in a split second. People who place too high a priority on being liked are often not the best choices for a project or company. A person who places high emphasis on people liking them often lose sight of the vision, purpose and cause of their firm. It's not that they should be disliked but being liked can't be a top priority of someone trying to be successful. I once interviewed a very smart computer programmer who had taken a train from the city for an interview. When I handed her the cards and asked her to lay them out, she very quickly asked for time to think about it. I said, "Sure, take your time. I'll be right back." I walked around the office and came back rather quickly. She was still arranging the cards, which indicated to me that she was over-thinking the chore and over-analyzing the "game." She was trying to win, which was good, but she was being totally left brained on the task.

Finally, we looked at the cards together. She had placed "to be liked" at the bottom of the deck. I asked her some basic questions and then focused on the last card, "I see you put 'to be liked' as the last card. Why?" She got intensely serious and said proudly, "I really don't care what other people think about me. I want to be judged only by my work." I quickly ended the interview.

About thirty minutes later she called me during her train ride back to the city. She was very contrite and asked, "I really messed up, didn't I?" I was polite and gentle when I explained the reason that her answer caused a problem. A team must work together in harmony and no one will be successful if those they work with don't like them. I wished her luck and that was that.

Now we come to the one card that throws off many people, "to be loved." Often this card raises the question, "Do you mean in my personal life or in business?" I reply, "Think of business. Of course, your family and friends outside of work already love you." Love is a wonderful emotion, and I have heard people who have been with a company for a long time say they love their co-workers. We had a General Manager who was proud to place "to be loved" as the first card on his stack. I asked, "You mean at work?" He had this gigantic smile on his face, "Yes, I want my people to LOVE me!" After talking to some of the people who worked for him, I learned that they did. This guy came in every morning and went to every worker and chatted about their kids, their work, their life, their hobbies and the like. Short of prying into their innermost emotional beliefs, this guy gave everyone so much attention they knew they were loved and in return they loved back.

I challenged him, asking why it was so important that he be loved. He explained that when people love you, they will do anything for you. They will work harder, always trying to make sure you are pleased. He added, "I didn't just love them, I motivated them to greatness." And judging by this guy's numbers, it was working. Well, until another company bought his unit and he was gone the next day. I guess money trumps love.

You should not treat the Douglas Test as the "end all, be all" way to find great people every time, but it's a great conversation starter during an interview and provides relevant insight about a candidate's personality. Over the years I have learned to be careful with generalizations. I have experienced people taking the test and after the discussion with me, wanting to redo their layout when they more fully understood its impact. That is only human and not at all bad. These folks want to fix things. They are problem solvers, always caring about their "permanent record." There is nothing wrong with that objective.

The process of hiring great people starts with a conversation. In a sense, the Douglas Test is just a trick. It's my attempt to get people to reveal something about themselves that could make a difference in my hiring decision. My only regret is that a person reading this book now knows how to beat the test, but winning isn't everything. They still must get through all the other challenges I will throw their way. If you use only one tool or idea when hiring people, you are hurting your company. Be creative and flexible, and always keenly observe the actions and reactions of your candidates.

8. Bring Someone Onboard

Much needs to happen between the time you've had your first interview with a candidate and the moment that new employee starts on the job. One of the most important duties of an employer is to check out the references of a potential hire. I was always intrigued when an applicant would list their "personal" references and then their "professional" testimonials. In my experience, rarely did the HR Department or supervisor call family or close friends to get an endorsement, but if someone on that personal list is a professional in your field you should probably reach out. I remember calling one reference and the person on the other end of the phone said, "I don't want to talk about him." That certainly caught my attention, and not in a good way!

With lawyers making so many decisions in our business world today, it's not unusual for the former employer of your potential new hire to deny access to that applicant's previous supervisor. Some employers have been instructed to provide only the employment dates, position held at the company, whether they are eligible for rehire, the reason for separation and perhaps a recommendation for another position or role, but all of that would be generous. Most companies verify only the dates of employment. Companies and their HR offices have become burdened with calls from creditors and banks, so they are now extremely cautious with their revelations.

In top government jobs, especially when security clearances are involved, the FBI or CIA will come to an applicant's house for an interview and probably chat with a few of their neighbors. Once the feds have a list of the applicant's associations, those people may also be interviewed. Everyone knows you should never lie to any law enforcement agents, but there are times a call from another firm to a former employer doesn't get much respect.

While I was writing this book, a news story came in about an Australian woman who lied on her resume and faked "glowing" references to land a high-paying job in a regional government office. When it was discovered she lied, the 46-year old woman was sentenced to one year in prison. The $185,000 job was snatched from her and she had to do jailtime. Truth matters.

I remember an occasion where one of the financial people at a company I was consulting was caught red-handed stealing money from the firm. To reduce the potential of costly litigation, the company demanded his resignation, gave him his earned bonuses and sent him packing. Now what happens when you call his former company for a reference on that guy? You get his employment dates and no reason for his departure. Had I answered the phone, I would have been tempted to say, **"Don't hire him, he stole money,"** but I could not say that because he could then sue me. There were no paper trails or court documents to prove the pilfer. So, why do we ask for references?

A useful tactic is looking at a candidate's reference list, which should always contain at least three names and try to figure out the relationship between the potential employee and those names on their list. Sometimes I would ask an interviewee, "So, this Joe guy here, was that your boss or just a friend?" Then I would simply listen, letting the candidate talk. The revealed details often helped me go further on a call with the reference of the person you are thinking about hiring. The old, "Hey Joe, I was talking with Harry about you today. You know, Harry Smith?" That tends to give you a better connection with the applicant's reference and just might loosen them up enough to provide more useful information.

The one thing you don't want to do is to give a potential hire the feeling that you are spying on them. At the same time, you owe your company due diligence when making decisions about personnel.

The number of investigative crime shows on TV is amazing. One show involved a serial killer "doctor" who did not have a medical degree but was working at a hospital. The plot revealed he was a violent, jealous husband who killed his wife after a dishonorable discharge from the army. We can only sit there and say, "Should have, could have, would have been avoided had they only checked the references."

As the debate continues about privacy and the revealing nature of the internet and social media, we can learn more about those around us and particularly those who want to work for us. For example, you can find a website that displays a map of convicted sex offenders in any neighborhood. We don't have the same technology to tell us who bounces checks or who is cheating on their spouse, but that could come in time. When hiring, you should judge not only a person's past but investigate what they are up to today.

I worked in a bed factory when I was in college. We joked about all the big guys who moved large furniture and mattresses on the third floor being ex-cons. I asked the owner about this one day, and he smiled and replied, "Some are, some are not, but they all work their butts off for me because they respect me for giving them a chance." The teaching moment was over. I learned a lesson about loyalty that day.

There are many achievement tests that can be administered to a potential hire after their first interview. If you are hiring someone for a job requiring an employee to carry and load 100-pound bags of salt on a truck, laws in your state may allow you to ask the applicant to demonstrate they have the physical capacity to do the work. A professional football team will ask a player to run the 40-yard dash because that is part of the job. Be careful, however. You cannot ask about physical disabilities. I once employed a Promotion Director who was paralyzed from the chest down. There were very few things he couldn't do, but I wouldn't have expected him to get down into a gully for a Civil War reenactment. One needs to be careful with physical limitations when interviewing. You might think a person in a wheelchair isn't as good for your company as the person who just ran the city marathon, but it would be unwise to make that conclusion before you study and learn about both people.

You might want to approach a prospective hire with the yardstick of education versus street smarts. You know age isn't important, but you still dwell on such a thing in your sub-conscious. You see someone young and might think, "fresh ideas," without testing their creativity on the spot. Every person is different and specific. Even identical twins have differences beyond the typical right hand/left hand concept. Don't be fooled by age or appearance.

One of the legally allowed questions you must ask is, "Why did you leave your last job?" In the radio business, the joke is that if DJs bought stock in U-Haul moving trucks, they would be rich by the ends of their careers. There are tons of turnover in the broadcasting business, mostly because of bad ratings. Another reason is lack of raises, so disc jockeys often move from station to station for a larger paycheck. The larger the market, the bigger the salary.

After you ask a question in an interview, permit the potential employee to state their case. Listen carefully and don't interrupt. If you're speaking with a candidate who worked for another company and is willing to discuss their experiences there, get every detail. If they go on a long disclaimer that sounds defensive, beware. I have interviewed applicants who completely trashed their old boss and previous place of work in five minutes. Remember, when they leave you, they very well might do the same thing to your company. Condemning a former supervisor and/or workplace is usually a bad sign and should be obvious that this person could bring their negative baggage into your business. The polite, "I separated on good terms, because the place wasn't a good fit for me," are the words of a person who will likely be able to forget about their bad experience and thrive in your company.

There are certain phrases I recommend you not use when interviewing and getting close to bringing a candidate into your firm or factory. I have heard the phrase, "…well, you are overqualified for this job," and was always miffed with the person who said it. If I apply for a job and the prospective employer makes clear the responsibilities of the position during my interview, why give me a "left-handed compliment" like the one above? I know someone who was being interviewed for a job when the interviewer said she should "be prepared to overcome her education." That statement is really saying, "This job is beneath you." If I were the applicant I would walk out immediately. People say stupid things. That's like a boss using this opening line of a salary increase negotiation, "You are severely overpaid here." Gee, can you make me feel any worse?

I was once interviewed at KDKA, the first commercial radio station in the United States and located in my hometown of Pittsburgh. I was applying for the position of Music Director when the Program Director asked what I saw myself doing in five years. I smiled and said, "I'd like to have your job." Okay, not smart. Yes, you are right, I didn't get the job. I am sure he thought I was overqualified. Because all employment and personnel consulting firms typically ask the same questions, candidates tend to give Miss America pageant type answers. There is nothing wrong with the, "Where do you see yourself in [insert number of years here]," question, but you must be able to do something useful with that information. If you can't use the answer, don't ask the question.

If a candidate's personal goals are in sync with your company and the open position, use that after you hire them to help them reach their specific goals. On the other hand, if it's apparent the job is just something the candidate will use to make money while they save for that sky-diving business they want to open, factor that knowledge into your decision making process about whether to hire them. It would probably be best to move on to another candidate.

At the end of any interview, you should ask the applicant if they have any questions. If you presented a twenty-minute history of your company, they may not have any big questions, but an interested candidate will pepper you with questions. The first might be, "What does this job pay?" and here's where the weasel factor in American business comes into play. Most times an employer knows exactly what they have in the budget and they probably aren't going to break the bank for a new hire. The interviewer might ask a candidate, "What kind of number are you thinking of?" This puts the applicant at a disadvantage. If the prospect asks you about money first, don't say it will be somewhere between this number and that number. That's a huge mistake. A possible future employee is going to want the top figure. Anything less than that sends the message that the candidate is not worth the highest rate. Often, an employer won't reveal the salary until they offer the job. This too is troublesome because you, as the employer, may be left at the altar if the number is too low. Then you've wasted your time and theirs. Why not simply state the starting salary and then lay out company policy about how long they must work to get benefits like vacation days and medical insurance? Being upfront is a great way to begin building a strong relationship with your candidate.

The golden rule is learning all you possibly can about a potential hire before bringing them onboard. You need to prepare for training them and they need your trust. They should feel as good about their decision to join your firm as you feel about your verdict to hire them. There are no guarantees that the marriage will work, but no matter what the future brings you will have a new family member on their first day of work.

9.   The Key to Training

There are three basic ways in which people learn. The first is reading about a process or task. Another involves watching someone else do the job then trying it on their own. Then there are those people who simply jump into the procedure, trying to figure out how it works as they go along.

The first learning method is much more logical and far less time consuming than the third. After all, if you must tear something apart so that you can put it back together the correct way, the task will take more time and the parts could become damaged from being used improperly. We all know about the person who gets a flat box containing pieces for a barbeque grill, ignores the instructions and "trials and errors" their way through assembling it.

Children learn how to speak and do things by watching their parents and mimicking them. When they get it right, the forthcoming acknowledgement and praise reinforces the lesson learned. There is no evidence that kids must learn how to eat dirt, they just do it. Through that and many other life experiences, they slowly learn that dirt tastes bad, that they shouldn't touch a hot stove and poking a large dog is not a great idea.

In today's complex business models, there is so much to learn beyond how to open the gate of the office parking lot and make your way to the front door. We get pictures taken for the company ID and sign a receipt for the electronic security fob. We learn the payroll and timekeeping software programs so we can get paid and request days off. We are instructed to watch online videos about sexual harassment in the workplace and we might have to take a governance exam that checks our understanding of company rules and policies. All of this typically happens before someone instructs us on what our day-to-day work entails and how to do it. Most larger companies have a policy manual that they make available and you should make sure everyone reads it.

There is so much going on in most companies that workers are hyper-focused on achieving their team's goals and they don't relish taking the time to train a new person. This is an attitude that must be dealt with immediately should it arise. Some companies give line workers an incentive for training and mentoring new hires. It makes sense that a new person who has acquired strong job skills could help co-workers more easily get the time off they deserve.

Some employees bring a distorted sense of ownership or unreasonable turfdom to their work. It's not productive if a staff member makes a newbie come to them for approval of each small step in a task. Most modern workers embrace new hires and don't foster that old-fashioned fear of the new guy taking their job. Fresh faces who have just been brought onboard often help lingering projects move along faster. In some businesses, there is a seasonal need for more workers, such as agriculture when additional people are hired for a large harvest. Tax preparation companies rush to get the work done before April 15th each year. These kinds of industries have an expansion and contraction built into their business plans and seasonal workers know they are temporary.

How to Hire Great People

American companies claim the investment to hire and train a new worker ranges from $10,000 to $60,000, so it's important to make sure you hire the right person. It's a terrible situation if you take on someone who appeared to be perfect for the position, but during the training process the key players on the team come to the conclusion the new employee doesn't have what it takes to learn and do the job. This is just one of the many reasons why you must be ultra-careful and inquisitive during the interviewing and hiring processes. Be aware of any hesitations and actions that make you question the capabilities of your candidate.

A smart company will quickly terminate a recent hire who isn't performing as the job requires. Yes, someone bungled the hiring procedures but why further hurt the company's performance just to protect a bad choice? I once hired a guy who had done a similar job at his previous place of employment. I assumed that he could do that same kind of work for me so I hired him, but he could not grasp the simple basics of the position he was to fill. I had to hire another person to fix the problem. I made a terrible mistake and the ordeal dragged on and on. We all make mistakes, but when it comes to an underperforming new hire it's important to cut your losses. Fix the situation quickly and then move on.

The software, medical and scientific businesses employ a process called peer-review, which was pioneered at universities across the nation. When a software developer writes code for a product, they will sit with another developer to show their work and explain their thinking about why they authored the code as they did. Often this process will uncover logic flaws or even code that crashes, but those kinds of issues now get found and fixed before they make their way into the product. The developers learn from each other and the practice improves the overall output of the team. This tutoring can also be handled by a supervisor who can critique and, if necessary, retrain certain aspects of the job.

Personalities always play a role in teamwork and a good manager will make sure an overly critical, tough task-master-type will not peer-review a more sensitive or timid co-worker. Fierce verbal putdowns can have lasting effects on certain fragile egos.

One summer, I worked in a steel mill in Pittsburgh. Us summer-job college students were warned about certain foolish ways of doing things from the sailor-language-barking, white hat bosses. Their approach was crude and overbearing but perhaps necessary to make sure we didn't fall into the strip steel acid bath and get pickled to death.

Many jobs in retail consist of repetitive, manual tasks, perhaps constant folding of the same merchandise multiple times a day, but that doesn't make such a job less important than any other. Some retail outlets place clothing or products in the same order and same location at every store. Other stores provide customers with apps so they can easily find what they need. It takes discipline to pull off the kind of work that must ensure a store's inventory is stocked according to plan. A crazy, outrageous, creative type who wants to go freeform in the workplace is not going to last long in an environment that requires structure and consistency. They can't just say, "I thought it looked better my way."

While researching for the writing of this book, I read about a famous energy company that now dominates the paper industry in America. I was surprised to learn about the number of employees who were killed working in their plants and warehouses over a ten-year period. To their credit, the firm took a hard look at their problem and discerned the reasons. First, mistakes were being frequently made by an overworked staff, fatigued from the use of too much overtime. Next, the company had placed unreasonable ultimatums on worker output, and their attempts to achieve unrealistic levels of production caused safety to be ignored, placing workers in harm's way. Another flaw in their system was training. Some workers were found to have adopted bad methods or applied shortcuts that were far too risky.

Here's an interesting story from my radio broadcasting days. A major company used a disturbing video to train radio engineers how to set up their remote broadcast vehicles at news events. Video and audio are sent from a remote location to a station's studio through a microwave transmitter. You've probably seen news trucks with their flashy logos and high tower antennas. Microwave transmission is line-of-sight, so the tower at the remote site must be raised high enough to align visually with the receiving dish at the station. Sadly, some broadcast workers have been killed when the tower is raised and meets electric power lines. In this training video, a man, whose family gave the company permission to use, suffered a horrible electrocution when he raised the truck's tower and it became fully engaged with high voltage electrical current from the overhead wires. Any person watching that video would have been sufficiently warned about what could happen if they make a mistake. The lesson learned in this case is you must always visually check out the surroundings before raising the tower.

The Occupational Safety and Health Administration (OSHA) sets federal guidelines for safe working environments and, barring egregious violations, the most dangerous thing most employees will encounter at work is bad mayo in the breakroom refrigerator. We'll talk more about OSHA later in this book.

A company and its executives must always be on the lookout for anything that might cause harm and, if found, get it fixed immediately. Along with new workers learning the company policies, it would be a good idea to have local fire prevention experts visit to explain the alarm system and evacuation procedures for your building. When I worked in White Plains, New York, every year the fire marshal's office held mandatory training sessions for office workers in every city building.

One of the greatest challenges in our high-tech world is that nothing stays the same. Just think about teaching yourself how to use your new cell phone. Even a software update can ground some companies for hours while they figure out the new interface, or worse, sort out the reasons why a critical application no longer works. Any company that doesn't keep in touch with today's quickly changing landscapes is destined to get lost. One of the great things about software programmers is they are pretty much full-on nerds and will spend hours of their own time learning new languages, protocols and tools because those things are fun to them. In other businesses, it might be learning that new-fangled automated mail machine or teaching the robot the company bought to replace you.

Young workers may take to change better than older workers, but you must make sure that age is not a factor when you make your decisions about training. One of the observations from a recently retired friend of mine is older workers are often more flexible when called upon to do tasks outside of their job description. She believes younger workers, who are rightly concerned about being taken seriously, will sniff at tasks they consider beneath them and tend to fret about how doing something outside of their job description impacts their image and productivity in the office. A more experienced worker who has been at the same company for a while will just go and get the mop to clean up the mess.

Don't assume every worker will take the time to learn a new process on their own simply because one nine-to-fiver surprised you by having the initiative to independently learn a new task or piece of gear. The internet houses millions of tutorials and one can find a video to learn just about anything, but a good manager won't fall into that trap. Some videos teach incorrect or harmful ways of doing things. When it comes to your company, determine the best training practices and make it mandatory for your workers to use the processes you have put in place. One basic no-brainer is a policy that any worker leaving their desk should log out of their computer, or at least lock it. Another key rule is any cell phone that is connected to your company network must be secured with a password.

We can't cover all the ever-changing aspects of business in our technology driven world, but you certainly should know about anyone not using the best practices of your firm and quickly rectify the situation. Imagine the person who leaves a VPN connection to your company's network open on their poorly protected home computer. That could give a hacker an easy way to enter your main server, partition off a large portion of same and start to serve pornography to the world using your hardware! I've seen this happen! In addition to slowing down your server, and thus your business, the legal implications are immense.

The initial instructions of a new person are only the beginning. As a manager, you must constantly update training on existing systems and hardware in addition to developing training schemes for new gear and processes. Also, the training of one employee means nothing unless you train everyone needing the knowledge. Perhaps we need a new word for training. People often think it has a beginning and an ending, a graduation of sorts, but good training involves constant and consistent intelligence gathering and updating. So, stop talking and start doing!

10. Money vs. Love

People used to ask me all the time if I liked my work and I had a standard reply, "I like 82% of what I do." What's funny is that no one ever asked what constituted the 18% I didn't like. Everyone knows that many job duties include tedious paperwork, unproductive confrontations and debates about things that really don't matter, that is, things that don't advance the agenda of the team, the group or the company. An important part of management is making sure all tasks and processes are relevant to company growth.

Once you hire your next superstar, you will soon learn the quirks and conundrums of that fresh new face. There is no way you can possibly know everything about a potential hire from resumes, interviews and special tests, but as the newbie starts to integrate with your systems, personnel and policies, a clearer picture about who they are will emerge. There are three reasons why you want to know what makes each of your workers tick: 1. Understanding the personality of every worker will help you to build effective teams. 2. Understanding the motivational hot buttons of your team members will help you properly reward their good work. 3. You need to see changes and potholes that might be demotivating factors and how to avert a disruptive or dangerous event before it happens. You'll want to establish a baseline for every person you manage and, of course, recall and reevaluate them as time goes on and your company history unfolds.

For example, we had a woman working with us who was deeply religious, and she started a spiritual relationship with a fellow worker.

Most of her co-workers viewed this liaison suspiciously and everyone saw her personality change. The relationship grew, probably into more than shared religious values, and this complicated the matter. Their religious practices seemed to be more cult than authentic, and many of the smart people around her avoided conversation, even as they were whispering behind her back that an intervention might be needed. When the company issued an ultimatum demanding that either she or her partner must leave the job, she decided to end the relationship. She realized that her professional achievements and bonding with her team were more important than running off with a lunatic into an uncertain economic future. Everyone rejoiced that her intelligence won out. The guy left New York for California.

Sometimes a person is totally motivated by a hobby outside of work, such as a father coaching his kids and their little league team. You may have such an employee working for you. Little league games often have early start times. To get to a 4 PM game, your employee might have to leave work early. You should be open to allowing that worker to come in early on game days or to make up the lost time in some other way. Should you be inflexible by not allowing your staffer to leave early, you will be eliminating an important aspect of his life, risking their loyalty to you and your company and perhaps pushing their motivation in a negative direction. Remember that common worker barb, "They don't care about me, so I don't care about them." If your structure is so rigid that it causes personal pain, you could very well turn a hard-working, productive person into a malcontent or drive them to seek a new job.

Some managers take the position, even though it is outdated, that work isn't supposed to be fun. Perhaps they make the stupid joke, "That's why it's called work." Let's get serious. People spend as much as 40% of their lives working, and a good manager will make sure that time spent in the workplace is not only productive but as enjoyable as possible. If a person was forced to work in a job they didn't like, they might consider it a form of slavery. Not all people get to freely choose their professions. Some are pounded into submission by their parents to work in the family business, or are forced to take over a company because of the death of a family member-owner. I imagine most workers who get pushed into a job aren't happy with the circumstance.

Many young adults place an emphasis on what they like to do as they pursue their first job. Some gravitate to pursuits that don't start out as jobs at all, like the young boy who plays basketball with the neighbor kids and, with a lot of work, becomes the best player on the block. Then he helps win the state championship for his high school. He goes on to college and becomes a well-known star and gets drafted by an NBA team. Then, for the first time, he is being payed money to play basketball, the game he loves. He never thought of playing basketball as work, but now that's his job. Few of us get to make millions doing work we love.

This brings up an interesting fact. It is unlikely you will ever fully understand the motivations of those you manage. Some people simply need to eat and will take any job that provides a paycheck. Perhaps that isn't the best reason for having a job, but some people who just want to get along in life can be excellent workers. Their motivation might make you question their seriousness about work, but be aware that people grow, change, learn and can become much more than what you, or even they, think.

Some people allow themselves to be consumed by work. I remember a time when I was managing workers in a state with a law stipulating that employees had to use or lose their vacation time by the end of the year. I would analyze the vacation schedules around the approach of the winter holidays and would invariably find one or two of my staffers had taken no vacation time. When asked about it, they said, "Oh, I just didn't have time because of all the work I have to do." They weren't speaking negatively. They were hard workers and totally dedicated to their role on their team, but not at all understanding the probable negative impact of not taking time off. People who don't take refreshing vacation time will eventually burn out and become less productive. Make sure your team members are fully utilizing the benefits of time away from the job.

We employ metrics to judge people, and the gradations often come in threes. For example, some people are hard workers, others might be productive but just putting in a minimal effort and a third assortment is occupied by lazy folks. There are talented employees, while others are limited but teachable, and then there are the poor souls who might be untrainable. We classify some workers as winners, others as fair-weather and we cast a shadow over those we consider to be losers. We hire leaders, we need followers and are observant to discover the rebels in the workforce. Some team members are natural innovators, others are flexible within rules and then there are the fixed position thinkers. Each of these types must be in the right places in your organization, and it's your responsibility to make sure they are and working effectively with folks of the other types. By the way, I would be remiss if I didn't plainly say that lazy or untrainable workers are liabilities.

We all know that work is work and that work is not play, and some of the common complaints we hear from people in the breakroom are not necessarily deep-seated desires to escape prison. After a person is on the job for a while, they tend to find fault with things that don't really matter, and there will always be several half-empty people in any group. Remember the Negative-Judgmental personality types will dwell on things they feel need to be better.

I worked at one company where the employees liked to eat popcorn at their desks. A problem arose when people didn't attend the microwave oven while cooking the popcorn and it burned. This set off the fire alarm, which automatically called the fire department. After several of these incidents, the fire marshal warned the boss that if this continued to happen the company would be fined. That was it, "No more popcorn!" For years people complained about the popcorn ban. Some corporate policies or rules will seem unfair to certain employees, but that's just the way it is.

As a boss, you will be faced with some hard choices. An employee who is chronically late to work can cause problems, even if their output is high in quantity and quality. Their team may be waiting to accomplish a task needing their contribution before they can proceed to the next phase. Workers also notice when a person is always late and begin to wonder if they have embarrassing photos of the boss. This disruptive behavior must be dealt with as soon as possible. Know that every person on your team feels strongly about the "fairness factor." When workers see others having an advantage they do not, morale suffers. If your employees believe things are impartial and equal in the work environment, the tightness of the team will be maintained and increased. Remember back to your grade school days when no one liked a "teacher's pet." If someone holds a co-worker in contempt, the goal of productive teamwork can fade away which would cast a negative reflection on your management. A great coach keeps the team together, even when there are disruptive members.

Many factors play into the way a person loves, likes or hates their job. It's not a simple one-size-fits-all concept. A constant managerial challenge for you will be deciding which tasks can be taken away from some employees while not making others pull more than their fair share. If you remove a disliked duty from a worker's job requirements, it's only fair you replace it with something else. You aren't there to make everyone feel good about everything. The adjustments you make must be based on productivity. If an employee reaches a breaking point, they may cross the bridge over to the island of the disgruntled. Once they land there, it's time for you to adjust their attitude or let them move on.

11.   Safety & Protection

There is something incredibly special about working, being paid a fair wage and having that grand feeling of accomplishing meaningful job and life goals. Researchers continually confirm that laborers who feel they control a significant amount of their jobsite destiny work harder and are more fulfilled than those who think just about everything involving their company is beyond their control.

There are specific policies, traditions and rules dictating how a worker is to perform in certain fields. In some workplaces, those rules come from unions or guilds. While the state has legislative power over the corporation, there is no way they can know what is happening at every moment in each company, including yours. There is no proof a government agency's oversight of all industries will keep you safe. Your company guidelines must be powerful enough to protect not only your employees but also the customers who use your product or service.

The story I'm about to share is all about one of the marvels of the 1950s when clocks and watches glowed in the dark. In those days, one could look down at their wristwatch at night and see the time without any light. For perspective, this was way before the genesis of light emitting diodes (LEDs). What was a magical innovation from the fifties came from the fertile brains of some smart inventors. When scientists developed a paint that absorbed light, and then emitted an eerie green glow, the watchmakers quickly applied this new technology to their clocks and watches.

The paint was based on radium, which emitted gamma rays that penetrated human tissue. The radioactive isotope was mixed with radio luminescent phosphor which produced visible light. Watch faces were covered by glass which kept wearers pretty much safe, but there was a different story for those crafting those glowing watches and clocks. Back in the days before automation, watch factory workers were mostly women and they painted the numbers and hands of a watch with the phosphor. Their bosses instructed them to routinely put the brush bristles in their mouths to make sure the tips were sharp for painting precision. Over time, many of those workers came down with cancer of the mouth and tongue because of the radioactive isotope in the paint. It took major lawsuits for the companies to admit this was the cause.

Fast forward to today and realize it's imperative that you keep your workers, customers and vendors safe. Most modern companies have excellent Human Resource departments where employees can turn if they have a question or problem. Large companies also have law firms to review contracts and procedures which protect the company and its workers. This is the cost of doing business in today's world. A mistake can cost a company not only millions of dollars but also its good will and reputation. The required legal retainers are worth every penny.

Working in the radio business has given me hundreds of stories that could fill an entire book, but one of them fits nicely into this chapter and it's a stark example of malfeasance. A radio station in Sacramento wanted to stir up some excitement by giving away a brand-new Wii video game system to one lucky listener. They came up with a contest named "Hold your wee for a Wii." As you will learn, someone obviously fell in love with the play-on-words rather than thinking through the entire concept. At a public event, contestants were asked to drink copious amounts of water and whoever lasted the longest without a bathroom break would win the prize. The woman who came in second died a few hours after the contest from what was determined to be "water intoxication." Often in life, too much of something can be harmful. Without dispelling water at a regular interval, a body can shut down, almost like an internal drowning.

The company that owned the radio station was sued and ended up paying the deceased contestant's family $16.5 million for wrongful death. In many TV shows where physical challenges or high-risk events are involved contestants are usually asked to sign detailed indemnification agreements, but why should any company take that kind of risk? When a business protects its customers, they also safeguard their employees from lawsuits.

As a manager, you've got to be careful that a well-meaning employee who volunteers to do something risky while on-the-job gets proper counsel. The excuse of getting something done faster is not going to protect you in court. Saying you didn't know that an employee was immersed in risky behavior will also not shield your company from possible lawsuits. Whenever there is a shadow of a doubt, contact your law firm for advice. I am not a lawyer, but over more than fifty years in business I've been involved with a significant number of lawsuits and court cases. I was an expert witness in many legal proceedings against broadcasters in which my primary job was to educate the judge about the traditions, policies and practices of the radio industry. No one wants to waste hours meeting with lawyers, preparing for lengthy depositions and mandated appearances in court. That's bad for business.

As either a worker or manager, you don't want to be the victim or scapegoat in a dispute. Here's a major fact. If a company can prove that only one employee was responsible for wrongdoing, that person will be sacrificed to avoid a big payout check. You don't need to be paranoid, but make sure you know the policies and rules of your profession. Should you begin to get tangled up in legal controversy, my best advice is to document in writing every event and your reaction or response. Yes, you might still get fired, but if you are a manager your responsibility is to protect your workers first, then your company and only then yourself and your employment status.

Safety and protection are interrelated with the points made earlier about training. It's crazy to me that major restaurants cause harm to their customers by not following basic Occupational Safety and Health Administration (OSHA) rules. A good manager will instill a sense of pride in workers who follow all the rules related to their business or industry. It's good for business and a great way for you to judge the moral grounding of every employee. For example, people who work in the food industry and don't wash their hands after a visit to the restroom should be weeded out and dismissed. People who steal rolls of toilet paper from a firm's stockroom each month should be terminated. Those kinds of things are not funny.

It takes a certain kind of commitment for an organization to look in every possible direction with an eye toward preventing a lurking disaster from happening. The old, faith-based axiom of "What's the worst thing that could happen?" doesn't fly in our modern world. This brings us to the balance between creating a positive, achievement-based working environment and making sure whistleblowers are not only protected but encouraged to come forward. Fear of retaliation from managers is no way to run a company, or a government.

Just as we encourage our workers to share their ideas to improve production and services, we should also embolden our employees to point out, even confidentially, when they see something in the workplace that could hurt the business or harm a worker. If the brakes on a truck are failing, an employee shouldn't feel they will be punished if they tell their boss something bad might happen. As a manager, you must act on any knowledge that could affect health and safety in your firm while never projecting negativity or blame on the complainant.

I want to mention again that all employees should feel safe on the job. Toxic workplaces are being exposed every day in America. Managers are obligated to disclose and deal with harassment, abuse, criminal activity or sabotage.

Companies are made up of people, and those people are assets. You wouldn't allow an employee to destroy a piece of company property, so why would you let any employee harm a co-worker? The success of a company is the basis for wages, benefits and raises. The more a business is successful, the more well-paid people it can hire, and this helps society at large.

There is a need for compliance and good governance in every company. You must protect your employees, customers and vendors. You are responsible for them. Safety and protection are paramount. Got it?

12. Recruitment & Public Relations

A company is much more than a building, a management structure and workers. I don't want to get too artsy here, but every company has an essence, a spirit, a shared-value system and a public face, intentional or otherwise, that is visible in everything it does.

I've seen extremely successful businesses that were forced to forfeit their reputations on painful calamities. The website Business Insider listed their picks of the *15 Biggest PR Disasters of The Decade*, and they aren't pretty.

They documented the Bridgestone tire debacle, in which the National Highway Transportation Safety Administration (NHTSA) linked nearly 200 deaths and more than 700 injuries to faulty tires, 6.5 million of which were eventually recalled by the company.

In 2000, preliminary studies showed that the painkiller Vioxx posed a potential heart health risk. Executives at pharmaceutical giant Merck did not pursue those studies. Four years later, Merck was forced to recall Vioxx because of evidence that it may have caused heart attacks and cardiac deaths of thousands who took the drug.

In the financial sector, all the executives of American International Group (AIG) flew private jets to a Congressional hearing in Washington after getting financial assistance from the federal government. Audacious? Yes! AIG got a bailout in 2008, then proceeded to host a $443,300 corporate retreat. The White House said this was despicable and made rules about the kind of retreats companies could have when receiving money from taxpayers, yet the stories continue.

One thing that bothers most Americans, and it should, is a notion of unfairness. In 2015, Martin Shkreli, the founder and chief executive of drug company Turing, decided to increase the price of the malaria and HIV medicine Darapim from $13.50 to $750. He was called to the US House Committee on Oversight and Government Reform to testify. Shkreli was widely reviled as the "Pharma Bro," because of his lack of empathy about customers being unable to buy his company's unaffordable medicines. This story had a good ending. Shkreli was convicted of trading fraud and got a seven-year prison sentence, but that hasn't stopped pharmaceutical companies from outrageous and unfair drug price increases.

Over my business career, I worked for good companies and bad companies. During my very first job as a newspaper delivery kid, I had a hundred customers, and during my years on the job I suffered through rough weather and dog attacks. I was an independent contractor of sorts, but there were rules I had to follow. The truck drivers who dropped newspapers at my home for delivery were members of the International Brotherhood of Teamsters (Yes, brothers. It was all men back then) and when they went out on strike, I didn't have a job. I learned salesmanship and gained a certain amount of confidence while folding, delivering and collecting payments for thousands of newspapers over the near decade. I also learned the expression *the customer is always right* wasn't necessarily true. I had several families move out of the neighborhood without paying their bills. My aggressive newspaper tossing broke several front door windows and I had to repair or pay for the damage. I was attacked by every type and breed of canine and never received much sympathy from the dog owners. Still, the years of delivering newspapers at doors and on porches gave me a sense of pride. As I grew older, my reputation became more important to me. I appreciated the Christmas presents, but never held it against any customer who didn't gift me.

The nature of how people think about you in business is always important. I used to make sure all the DJs and promotion people at my radio station understood that they must never do anything stupid when they were out in public, such as driving around town in the radio station van. Cutting off another driver and flipping them the bird could lose a listener. This concept is even more important in today's big, bad world of business. We now have social media, which can cause the loss of legions of customers with a single misstep.

My doctor once called me and, knowing about my internet expertise, asked how she could get rid of a bad review on Yelp. The matter stemmed from a patient who didn't understand the doctor's payment policies, which required him to cover whatever his insurance didn't. Now I am extremely sensitive and vocal about healthcare, and it's disturbing that we often don't know the cost of a procedure or medication until we get the bill, but this specific case was due to the patient's misunderstanding. The vitriol in his online critique might have made him feel better, but his takedown was one-sided and more than unfair. I explained to my doctor that many websites with customer comments arrange them chronologically, and I suggested she solicit positive reviews from other patients to push the disgruntled customer's comment further down the list. However, not all sites work this way, and some of the better ones let you search by negatives, positives or keywords. A good manager will search for reviews of their company's products or services and do their best to manage any negative or unfair comments. There are times a well-worded reply can completely remove the sting of a negative review. The reach and power of the internet demands that you keep a watchful eye on everything said there about your business.

Your company's reputation is extremely important. When you are recruiting, you will find smart people who keep an eye out for opportunities and know how to intelligently and effectively use the internet to help chart a path toward their new job. When I am looking for a company to help my firm with a project or service, I first research about them on the Better Business Bureau site. I know, I know this seems old-fashioned, but I want to know if any people were motivated enough to file a complaint after having a bad experience. Yes, I sometimes see silly complaints, but when I am about to spend my company's money I will wade through all the information I can find to make an informed decision.

I would never go to work for someone like Martin Shkreli, nor would I apply for a job at a company that had major disputes with their workforce. If you know a company has been fined for bad behavior, it would be wise to research the situation and that firm's management before interviewing there. A business that has been charged with discrimination or any other negative matter is probably not a place where you want to work. As a manager, you must always be aware of and protect your company's image.

It's important for a company to engage in productive public relations to make sure its consumers and future employees think they are good actors. You see lots of corporate ads on Sunday morning TV talk shows because those sponsors want government officials to believe they are reliable and honest. Many companies support public radio and public TV stations to foster an image of community orientation and involvement.

Recently, there were some negative stories on TV and social media sites about the working conditions at Amazon warehouses and shipping centers. Amazon is a large company, and it quickly addressed these negatives by running advertisements showing happy workers talking about how great it is to work at Amazon and touting the benefits the company offered. Full disclosure here: Kindle Direct Publishing handles all my books. I have never had a complaint about their involvement with my book publishing but, to be clear, I am not an employee.

The impression of "biggest" is an important aspect of American commerce. We have a growth concept in the United States which is based on large companies buying little companies. Slowly the competition gets compressed into two or three giants. We have laws in America that attempt to preserve competition, and while they are helpful they do not prevent monopolies. There are fewer competitors in many industries and product lines. For example, there's only one Major League Baseball, there's only one satellite radio company and now we are down to three major cell phone companies. Big is the American way.

Working for a large company has its advantages. When my software company was owned by only a few individuals, it was necessary to borrow money from banks for major expansions. After the business was bought by a mega-media company, it was able to multiply faster but then had to make a bunch of money to keep the stockholders happy.

There is a good question about how much employees should share in a company. We will amplify this later in a chapter on keeping good people, but it's important that you instill a feeling of success and positive future outcomes in each of your employees. If they think your firm is on shaky financial ground, they will start to look around for a company that appears to be more stable. It's basic human nature.

Here's a solid tip from this discussion of public relations and how it applies to recruitment. You should ask each prospective employee, "What do you know about our company?" Lots of interviewers fail to do this, and they miss an important and vital link to finding the right person. It's bad on two levels if a prospective hire says, "Oh, I don't know anything. The first I heard about your firm was seeing the help wanted ad." One reason may be that you aren't as visible a company as you should be. The other area of concern is the candidate didn't take the time to research your firm. In the case of the former, it might be time to evaluate your public relations (PR) and marketing. As for the latter, if the candidate wasn't motivated to research your company what might that say about their motivation should you hire them?

Remember, being famous or being infamous is not public relations, it's publicity, and there's a big difference between the two. Perhaps you have heard of the company ENRON, and while it existed you might have thought it was the greatest company in the country. However, we now all know it was the very worst place to work. Not all companies think of recruitment when they advertise their products and services and I get that, but it's wise to always keep long term goals at the top of your mind. What is the overall image of your company on the street? Is it a glowing impression or are there many dark shadows?

People are mostly objective. If a business had one or more big problems in the past, it may have shaken up the management and publicly promoted its solutions. With all the purges in the media business because of the #MeToo movement, I'm sure people now feel that NBC and CBS have become better places to work. This doesn't mean that those companies can stop promoting their team spirit, healthy work environments and benefits delivered. It's an ongoing effort to balance the fatigue of a workforce against the need to constantly refresh and move forward with progressive ideas. Bringing in new people is one possible solution. New hires often have inspiring and workable ideas for positive and effective company changes.

Whether you use the internet or you network with face-to-face gatherings to find employee candidates, it's important keep your brand in front of recruits. I always encouraged my employees to attend industry conventions and meet as many people as possible. Some bosses are paranoid about sending their best people out to a business event because they fear other companies will lure them away, but that's not a productive attitude. If your workers are that susceptible to being hired away, then you aren't doing a good job of keeping them. You should be fostering a partnership type of relationship with your employees so they will not leave your firm and they will refer good people to you.

Print ads, which were the backbone of job searching in the past, are no longer in major use. To underscore this point, the newspaper I delivered all those years ago no longer exists. We mentioned headhunters, and in some specific industries they are the best way to bring new people to your organization. Professional societies that sell ads for recruitment in their newsletters and websites can also be highly effective in helping to fill openings.

The key to successful advertising is creating an effective message that properly images your company and describes the open position. Advertising is just as important as PR. Whatever you do, please don't use lame humor. I once saw an ad that said, "Losers need not apply." Who wrote that? I also have a big problem with the words "NO CALLS PLEASE." It stems from a weird belief that somehow phone calls will clog the system. When you welcome telephone contact, you increase your chances of finding a great prospect. The worst thing a potential employee could hear from you is, "WE DON'T WANT TO TALK TO YOU." How is that good public relations? What image does that send to a prospective hire? Think about it. When a person is unemployed and in need of a new job, they are probably a little insecure and majorly fatigued by rejections. Why add to their frustration if all they want to do is ask a question? By the way, that question you are trying to avoid answering is probably what the job pays. Why would a job hunter want to waste their time on a minimum wage position if they are an experienced worker in a highly paid craft? By accepting the call and answering such a person's question about salary, you spared yourself and the candidate an interview guaranteed to go nowhere.

Successful recruitment is based on the public persona and perception of your company. Don't ever be too busy handling all the other aspects of your job that you fail to wear a bright face and polite aura.

13.   No Surprises

I once worked with a quirky radio executive named Bob Reich. He was the General Manager, the top dog, of his radio station. Besides being a successful broadcaster, he had another claim to fame. His son was a kicker for the 1987 University of Tennessee football team. I first learned this because there was a picture on Bob's desk showing his son kicking the winning goal in the opening contest that year against Iowa in the "Kick-off Classic Game." That picture was motivational because his son, Phil, was not recruited by the team. He surprised the coach with a walk-on tryout and excelled to the degree he earned a spot on the team. He got his shot on the field when its highly touted kicker was injured and, as they say in sports, the rest is history, but let's get back to his dad, Bob.

Most people imagine running a music radio station is a lot of fun, and while there certainly are many enjoyable aspects to the job it's a serious, complicated affair. First, many people must like what you put on the air enough to listen, which generates ratings. The things most listeners don't like — the commercials — are sold to advertisers so those ratings can be turned into gold. Advertising is the primary way a radio station makes money. If the ratings are low, the station will most likely lose money and the entire staff may get fired and/or there may be a format change for the station. I am sure you have experienced the strange phenomenon of turning on the radio one morning to find that your favorite station is gone. It could be what was your favorite smooth jazz station now has a new name and is playing hip hop music. Maybe the previous format didn't get ratings, the sales department wasn't working efficiently to generate revenue, or a new owner simply wanted to start from scratch with something new.

Great radio managers are involved with not only the product on the air, but they also motivate those souls who bang on business doors to bring home the bacon. I have seen one station with great ratings do well in sales with casual selling and taking orders, while another less-rated station's sales exceled by using creative selling propositions and personable pitches.

Bob Reich always puts together a solid team of salespeople and managers at stations under his wings. Whenever Bob began work at a new station, I would attend his first sales meeting which always included a mantra. There was a time I thought his directive was kind of silly, but the more I heard it and thought about it the more I came to understand its good sense. It went something like this, "Here at [insert station name], my policy above all else is NO SURPRISES!" Now what the heck does that mean?

Many employees try to psyche themselves up for the day ahead as they make their way into work. They may be stressed while driving through terrible traffic or they might be dealing with problems at home, but they're doing their best to get to their workplaces in good headspaces with the least amount of anxiety. An employee who works in a highly charged, demanding environment may use their time in the car to mellow into a Zen-like condition which will help them through the next eight hours. With all this in mind, the last thing an employee wants is some sort of surprise when they get to work.

The revelation that your manager, in a fit of anal-retentiveness, made someone throw out all the old food and condiments in the breakroom refrigerator over the weekend, including what was to be your lunch, can be disturbing. This is a great example of what "no surprises" is all about. A good manager will always share important issues with workers to make sure their expectations are considered and maintained. Had the boss sent out a note that said, "Hey, the refrigerator purge is coming over the weekend. Take home whatever food you want to keep or it might be gone on Monday!" That kind of thoughtfulness would help people cope. By the way, the concept of "no surprises" works both ways. You should always do your best to present no surprises to your boss.

I have been involved in several business situations where, after productive decision-making meetings with stakeholders, I was quite surprised to see things unfold in ways different from what the team decided. After asking, "How did this happen?" I was astonished to hear, "Oh, we decided to do it another way." Really? Sometimes, without the constant reminder of "no surprises," people begin to "call audibles." This is a football term describing a situation in which the quarterback is given a play, but he calls a different one at the line of scrimmage. You might give a quarterback that kind of flexibility because he may see the defense in a vulnerable alignment, but in business you generally don't want to have any action based on a whim.

Here's a great story about the Gateway Arch in St. Louis. The pieces were made in Pittsburgh, floated down the Mississippi River and then placed on the shore. The monument was designed with microprecision and the builders had to follow a strict plan without any surprises. Before the last piece was to be put into place, the Mayor demanded that it occur on a day different from the original plan. The Mayor called an "audible." On that day, the temperature at the base of the arch where the last piece was stored was much warmer than the temperature at the top of the arch. When the final piece was hoisted up, it didn't fit because the heat had expanded it. The 630-foot arch ceremony could have been a complete embarrassment for the city fathers that day, but the engineers came up with a brilliant idea. They summoned the fire department to hose down the non-fitting piece with cold water. The metal cooled and shrank, and eventually the final piece was neatly fitted into the gap at the top of the arch.

Yes, all the planning in the world might give you confidence, but that takes someone analyzing every piece of data and asking all possible "what if" questions long before the day of execution. I like to turn the "no surprises" mantra into the possibility that surprises could be lurking somewhere in the design, somewhere in the very people who must do the job or somewhere in the policies of a company. This makes it essential that you always keep the team on your side. Make sure they have the courage and power to alert you of any potential "pop goes the weasel" moment that could make a project implode or collapse.

There are some rules about process that make sense in this scenario. Rehearsals and practice are of supreme importance. You can't practice something like placing the final piece of an arch, which is a one-time shot, but you can work with small models and test theories in the lab. I was impressed with work once done at Harvard involving the assessment of an experimental drug. The lab workers grew a patient's cells in a petri dish and then introduced the drug to those cells so they could evaluate the outcome without using that drug on the patient.

Sometimes you have time to examine your concept as it's being completed, but many times, corporations don't want to spend the money on pre-testing. All new ideas are risky, but there can be pleasant surprises like the discovery that rheumatoid arthritis medicine also thwarts psoriasis. Engineer Percy Spencer had a wonderfully great surprise at the Raytheon Corporation in 1946. A chocolate bar in his pocket melted while he was testing a new vacuum tube, and this led to the invention of the microwave oven.

Systems are put in place for safety or efficiency and people who try to step around them can slow progress, or worse, kill themselves or others. I like to think that Bob's "no surprises" radio guideline was an overarching rule which involved much more than simply doing the job. If a radio DJ got drunk at a station promotion and decided to rip the mirrors off the competition's van, Bob expected to hear about it from his staff instead of reading about it in the newspaper. Surprise! Surprise! If you are stern and militaristic in the way you treat your people, you may create a "don't ask, don't tell" atmosphere. Your employees could become so terrified of being yelled at when presenting you unwanted news, they won't tell you important variances of conduct or corruption. A great leader inspires trust and confidence in their teams so members will feel at ease, even when they need to disclose unwelcomed information.

Always look at things through the eyes of your workers. They don't want their workplace leader to be inconsistent or capricious. I remember one of my bosses yelling and screaming during a phone call with me and several other loyal employees. He wanted us to fix a problem and was screaming like a drill sergeant at Parris Island, but his demands were incoherent. Finally, there was a pause and the senior-most guy on the phone asked, "Who were you talking to?" The boss barked, "Whoever was listening!" before slamming down the phone. We needed a separate call amongst ourselves later to figure out who would do what. Much to the boss' surprise, we crafted a way to resolve the problem without him.

One concept I learned while working in software fits neatly into this chapter. You cannot always avoid surprises, but you can manage expectations. People get hell bent that things must go a certain way. They may have a "wishful thinking gene" which drives them to believe everything must follow their vision to yield a satisfactory outcome. The smart supervisor will be predictive and manage the expectations of those above him, so a less than great result will be taken in stride. Should some wise guy on the team boastfully claim we could do something in a few days, when the rest of the team knows it will take several weeks, simply be honest. Spare the boss the unpleasant surprise of an unrealistic timeline. Doing so will lessen the chance of him or her blaming the whole team instead of the single person who dreamed a quicker result.

You know that you and your team must all work together, and no man is an island, but there are times when you must say, "Please, do it this way." Don't say, "**Do it my way**," because that comes off like the parent who pulls the "because I said so" card out of the authority deck. Believe it or not, I've heard that one followed by the old, "Well, I own the company and some day when you own a company you can do it your way." What a downer. It's basically saying a worker's ideas will be valid only when they are an owner or high ranking executive. Being a manager is hard enough, but don't make it more difficult than it is. Make sure you don't zap motivation with your words. You may be surprised how well positivity promotes productivity.

14. Crisis Management

The topic of crisis management was in the outline I created for this book, but I didn't flesh it out originally because I was hesitant about its relevance. Then, something terrible happened. A global pandemic struck. A virus began spreading around the world at breakneck speed. Alarmingly, we had no vaccine or known treatment, and about 1% of the people who contracted it died. COVID-19 and all that came with it shined a completely different light on the topic of crisis in my mind, and this chapter is the result.

The best advice during the global pandemic was a "social distancing" campaign. Not only did this prevent people from working, it caused the world economy to grind to a halt. Stores and businesses closed and everyone was asked to self-quarantine at home. Most companies and medical facilities were simply not equipped to deal with this intense crisis.

Now, let's back up a bit. When we hire great people, we want to do everything we can to protect them. Not only are we legally obligated to keep them safe, but we are morally driven to do the right things, both small and large.

The revenue stream of a radio station is derived mostly from the commercials played over the air. Each advertisement is paid for by a business, and when a commercial is not played, for whatever reason, the station doesn't get paid. I was in Charlotte, North Carolina on a bright, sunny day where I was meeting with a radio client. After arriving at the radio station, the very gregarious General Manager gathered a group of us saying we'll all go out and he will buy us brunch.

As we walked to the restaurant, I saw a bunch of city workers digging a rather large hole in one of the Queen City's main downtown streets. I didn't think much about it, until the electricity went out just as the food arrived at our table. We all chuckled a bit in the diminished light but enthusiastically dug into our meals. The manager's cell phone rang right then, and I watched his face turn white as he listened to the voice on the other end of the line. He abruptly ended the call and said, "Bad news, we've got to get back to the radio station. The power is out." In the radio business, when you have no electricity you have no radio signal, and when you are off the air commercials aren't broadcast and money is lost.

As we walked back to the station's studios, I turned to the manager and asked, "The station has a power generator, right?" He just shook his head and explained that they had a generator at the transmitter site on the mountain, but not at the studios. He further explained, "Another generator was going to cost $19,000 and I took it out of the budget." So, there he was, no power, no generator and the station was losing around $11,000 each hour due to commercials which couldn't be broadcast. The station was silent for two hours, losing more money than that generator would have cost. The manager gambled and lost. Two hours was a relatively short time; it could have been much longer.

When I worked at a radio station in Atlanta, a wicked tornado tore through town and toppled many trees over electric lines causing a widespread power outage for three days. We did have a generator and it kept the radio station on the air for two days, before it needed more gasoline to keep going. No electricity means gasoline pumps don't work, so we had to find gas from another source, which we did. However, there was a much larger problem. Yes, we were on the air and playing those commercials, but the generator powered only the broadcasting equipment; the air conditioning was not running. The Hotlanta sun beat down on our radio studios and the windows to the outside world could not be opened. An open window in a radio studio leads to outside noise being transmitted over the air, so the windows in many broadcast facilities are often unopenable, fixed panes of glass. Our studios got unbearably hot. The DJs were real troopers, doing their shifts with practically no clothes on, but it was an extremely dangerous situation and we were breaking US labor laws by making them work under those conditions. We should have had a small remote studio at the transmitter site or a larger power generator to run the air conditioning at the studios.

I worked at a radio station in Pittsburgh which was in a high-rise building downtown. One night, the building caught on fire and, as smoke filled the studio, I had to argue with the disc jockey about leaving the facility. He didn't take it seriously. When firemen with big axes arrived, he finally got the message and left.

Always remember that whatever can go wrong — will. You know, it's Murphy's Law. The best advice I can offer you is to call together a free-lunch meeting with your most creative thinkers and brainstorm a list of every possible problem that could happen in your workplace. What would you do if there was an active shooter in the office? What about a fire? A flood? A power loss spanning days? And now, yes, a pandemic. After creating the doomsday list, construct a solution for each one designed to save lives while keeping the business safe and running, and then create a "playbook."

People who know me always shake their heads when they hear one of my stories. Perhaps it's my age, or some strange karma that has attached itself to me, but there are countless times I find myself in the most unusual, sometimes utterly bizarre, situations. On April 29, 1992, I was working with KABC radio in Los Angeles. I remember going into the newsroom of that famous News/Talk station with about a dozen employees. On the TV, while our announcers where covering the same event, the anchor spoke of the verdict in the case against three Los Angeles police officers who were charged with beating Rodney King while trying to arrest him. That incident was caught on camera and was shown again and again on both local and national news shows. The officers were found not guilty, and I could feel the tension in the room. The Hispanic and African American employees were amazed the officers were acquitted, while the Asian and White employees knew things were going to get bad.

Bad it got, with riots and looting taking place all over the city. KABC is on La Cienega Boulevard, and next door to the facility was a furniture store that got looted and firebombed, causing it to burn to the ground. The General Manager of the station acted quickly by hiring armed Pinkerton guards with machine guns and he directed them to the station's roof to keep evil actors away. I was ordered out of the station that night, and the normal 30-minute drive to the airport took more than three hours. Most of the employees who were in the building stayed there, broadcasting 24 hours a day to a city in ruin, which brings us to your disaster planning.

Could employees stay in your office or plant 24/7 if they had to? Do you have cots and blankets on your premises? Could food be stored and cooked in your establishment? You might think that is asking too much but, as Murphy reminds us, you never know.

I was working for a software company in New York on 9/11 and remember the techies struggling to get us back to the internet. To keep up with the happenings in the City, we grabbed an old TV and fashioned a makeshift antenna using a length of wire. We kept the office open for hours after the attacks, but some of our employees knew people who worked in the World Trade Center and it quickly became apparent that concentrating on work was impossible for us all. We closed early in the afternoon on that frightening day, but not before a great idea backfired.

The HR department wanted to help people face their dark feelings and despair, so they put together what was supposed to be a brief grief counseling session in a conference room. In attendance were several employees of the Muslim faith, and one hardliner xenophobe began to spew venom about why the attacks happened. Here was a case of trying to do the right thing, but circumstances took good intentions to a bad place.

Crisis management is probably the hardest thing a manager or employer must deal with, and there rarely are easy answers. To hire great people and keep them, you've got to tap into their strengths rather than dictate what you believe to be true. When in doubt, show some love and respect, bring in some food and ask them what they need. It could be that a worker must deliver packages that might be covered with a virus or poison. Give them the masks and gloves they need to do their job. They shouldn't have to bring in supplies from home to keep safe while working.

We have learned a lot from the COVID-19 pandemic. When a clearly articulated plan is in place, people will rise to the cause and need and everyone will pitch in to confront something bad that affects many. We saw it during 9/11 and we saw it with the pandemic. You must instill a sense of confidence and show people the light at the end of the tunnel. In our sweltering Atlanta radio studio with no power, we brought in fans to blow air on the DJs and tubs of ice packed with beverages. Okay, there were also some beers in there but hey, it was a crisis.

As part of your crisis preparedness, factor in solutions that can be handled while working from home. Yes, some jobs cannot be done offsite, but if you can protect most of your workers from a dangerous location or situation please plan for it. With innovations like cloud computing networks and web-based software, you may be able to adapt quickly to a crisis. Perhaps the ideas in this chapter will help you keep those great employees around for an even longer time.

I was amazed by how many of the restaurants that closed during the coronavirus crisis were not equipped for takeout or delivery. They were not prepared for the crisis that hit them. Some were just too small to make ends meet with only takeout food, while the employees of others were so frightened by the crisis they simply didn't come to work. Consider these possibilities and how you would handle them as you write your playbook.

Make sure to consider all of the hard questions that need to be answered in every disaster scenario. Is your company adequately insured to cover loss or injuries to employees, and does it offer adequate medical coverage? If such inquiries are above your pay grade, direct them to and get answers from the responsible parties. What would you do in a mundane crisis, such as being hacked, or having all your systems go down? Does everyone at the plant know what their job is under the various circumstances?

We learned painfully the one question hardly anyone wanted to ask during the global pandemic, "Does the business NEED to be up and running?" What is your playbook for a reduced workforce in a contracting business model? If you must shut down the business, do you know the difference between furloughing staff and terminating workers? A furlough is "a temporary layoff from work," while most of the time a furloughed employee doesn't get paid, they do keep employee benefits such as health insurance. People who get furloughed usually return to their jobs after the layoff ends.

When a crisis hits, watch your people closely. Some of your team members will blossom, and they could very well be your future leaders. Frontrunners take charge during dark days.

15. Firing & Quitting

I have often said that no one knows how to quit a job and no one knows how to be fired. With those thoughts, let's take a deep and honest look at two of the biggest challenges of workplace separation.

This book is written mostly for managers and I won't overstate the worker's perspective, but as a supervisor you should walk a mile in their shoes. Most people take a job with the idea of staying with their new company for as long as possible. There are those of us who have been in a position of knowing we were soon going to leave our company but made the mistake of telling too many people about their upcoming move. I know one person who talked about retiring, and when her boss heard about it from another, he took her out of the budget for the following year. That was bad news for both involved because she was talking about retirement two years ahead. Ouch! The mistake was resolved, but here's the important lesson to all; keep your mouth shut.

I once was in a position where the guy hiring me for another job was a good friend of my current boss, and without my knowledge or permission he told my boss I would be leaving at the end of the year. One day I came to work and was told to train a guy waiting in the lobby. When I asked what position he should be trained for, my boss said, "Your job." It eventually did work out, but not on the timetable I wanted. After getting down to the last few dollars in my bank account three months later, I finally was able to start my new job.

Normal business ethics require you to give your company at least two weeks' notice before leaving their employ. Some companies demand more advance notice. Depending on the specifics in a contract or agreement you may have with the company, your departure should at least follow the traditions and rules of your specific industry.

Much of what happens in the radio business is action packed, emotional and crazy. There are many stories about fired radio disc jockeys nailing their shoes to their boss's office door with a sign that reads, "You'll never fill these." Not only did those former employees have to pay for new doors, they also ruined perfectly good shoes.

One of my lawyers shared his story of the "Yom Kippur caper," where all the non-Jewish attorneys moved out of his office on that holiday and started a competing law firm across the street. Yom Kippur, also known as the Day of Atonement, is the holiest day of the year in Judaism and he used to always say, "I hope those S.O.B.'s atoned for their sins of walking out."

Most managers don't have a "what if" plan should certain members of their team quit, but they should. Corporate people know it doesn't happen often, but you would be loyal and true to your employer to think about backup plans and strategies to replace important workers should they suddenly leave. It's a similar approach to what companies do when facing the possibility of an organized labor walkout. Who will run the plant? It's your responsibility to keep the business moving forward. If you sense things will grind to a halt, you need to think about stockpiling product for the impending slow down or lock out.

I have always been a bit skeptical of an employee who comes in and says, "Hey boss, it's time for me to make a move." When I ask how soon they will leave, they reply, "Oh, two weeks or less, if that would be okay?" I then probe to find out where they are going. I never do this in a confrontational way, realizing they are probably quite nervous about letting me know the issues surrounding their departure. As much as you might feel emotional about their leaving, there is one important thing you need to know. Are they going to work for a competitor? If they are bold and blurt out they're going to be working for your arch enemy, you need to forgo the two-week notice and get them to HR for an immediate exit.

When learning an employee is going over to the "dark side," some companies disallow that worker to gather their personal belongings from their office. That's a bit much, but I do recommend that an HR person go with any departing employee as they gather their personal possessions. Things happen fast these days, and a firing requires you to be cautious. You don't want a person who just got dismissed going from desk to desk to bring down others. I remember an early morning when a major executive at my place of business was terminated. I found the IT guy in my office asking me why Joe Blow's email account was terminated a few minutes ago. The techies are usually the first to know about employee changes because they control the email system and the server permissions of all employees.

When someone who is particularly loved and admired in the workplace gets fired or quits, it's going to affect many people. If they are fired, their co-workers will want to know why. If they quit, people will discuss why that person was not happy. I have also seen a strange process where people start to scavenge the office of a departing employee. "Oh, he had a great stapler. I'll take that." I remember a time when a worker about to leave the company was in the HR office making his exit arrangements, while another employee was in his office hauling out the white board, easel and all the colorful markers he used for presentations. When the guy decided not to leave, he had to retrieve his equipment from his overzealous co-worker.

As a manager, you need to develop a consistent and fair way to handle things when one of your team members quits or gets fired. They are not the same thing, but the net result to the team can be. You or someone you designate needs to know what the person was working on and what needs to be picked up by other team members. This reminds me of the story about a new manager at a radio station in Tallahassee, Florida. Coming into the offices and studios for the very first time on an early winter morning, he noticed the light over the front door was out. The light remained out on his second and third days, so he asked the receptionist about it. She smiled and said, "Oh, the bulbs are in your desk. The former manager always took care of that." He had no idea that basic maintenance was part of his job.

Firing people is not fun. I had to dismiss someone when I was young and just starting out in management and confronted a strange malady. Right in the middle of this firing, I wanted to start laughing. It was a strange nervous tick I had to suppress. Fortunately, for most today the termination of an employee is usually done by an HR executive, but if you are the manager you will be involved in that final meeting.

It can be difficult when the person being fired asks, "Why am I being let go?" Your kind nature, especially if you have a great business relationship with the person leaving, may compel you to give the person a detailed explanation about why they are being let go. STOP. With the way labor laws and wrongful termination lawsuits have progressed in this country, you could do major harm to your company trying to explain this worker's terrible fate. It's best if you leave that responsibility to the HR department. They will know the details of termination and have guidance from the lawyers about the proper language to use.

You will be pouring gasoline on a smoldering fire should you say something like, "Well, you know, the boss never really liked you." That's not a reasonable explanation to give to someone going through such a terrible ordeal. Some good responses are, "Well, we just wanted to make a change," or, "We're reorganizing," or "We're downsizing," or, the big lie, "We're going in a different direction." Unless you have a video of the person stealing stuff from the company storage room, you don't need to regurgitate the sins of the soon to be dearly departed.

Let's look more closely at the issue of being terminated for cause. This is typically misunderstood by many young managers. Basic fairness principles have been written into our country's labor laws and it's important that you always create a proper paper trail. A good manager will discuss each instance of an employee's misbehavior with them and follow it up with a memo placed in their file which details the infraction and summarizes the dialogue about it. You cannot make stuff up. What you claim must be real and should be backed up with evidence you did everything you could to help the employee improve and curtail their poor behavior. Never use spiteful or vindictive language in the improvement suggestion reports.

Over the years, judges and juries have seen some incredible hatchet jobs in the workplace. You cannot harass an employee into leaving. In the past, it wasn't unheard of for a disc jockey to move 800 miles on their own dime to take a job, only to run afoul of a manager a few days after arriving and be assigned to an overnight shift, in the hope that the new hire would quit. That's not a proper way to do it, and I am proud to tell you the radio business has decidedly cleaned up its act over the years, but such ploys still happen in businesses across the land. The boss may remove high profile clients from the primo list of a veteran salesperson, hoping the drop in commissions will motivate her to pack her bags. This is not good business.

The annual reviews of employees to give feedback and direction have created common grievances about waiting until the end of the year to tell workers how to improve. Why not point out lapses immediately? Another gripe arises when workers are told their annual reviews have no impact on salary. Really? If the review has nothing to do with compensation packages, then why are we doing them?

I feel annual reviews should cover an employee's goals, challenges and accomplishments from the previous year and detail expectations for the new year ahead. If I saw an employee struggling with some part of their job or performance, I would encourage them to seek further education as a goal to help them. Some companies will pay for such additional education. Sending an employee to a three-day seminar can help them learn and be a motivating experience. I always loved it when a worker would bring back great new ideas from their training and share with the rest of the team the concepts or innovations they learned.

You've got to find that magic button inside every employee that inspires them to strive. They should never carry performance fear into their day-to-day tasks. I'm sure future Hall of Fame quarterback Tom Brady doesn't go into games with fear of failure. He knows he can improve but doesn't get overly emotional when he can't produce. He just focuses on the next game. What are you going to do tomorrow to make your team work better?

A major part of your responsibility as a manager is self-improvement. There are seminars about how to motivate a team and workshops covering the legal aspects of dealing with employees. You may not think about how you are going to fire someone on the day you hire them, but perhaps you should. I've had the experience of a person coming back to me later in their life to thank me for firing them. "Hey, you were right! I was lazy, and you got me to consider another path." I am sure there are others out there who have a Dwight Douglas "voodoo doll" they stick needles in every night.

There is one stark reality. If you don't fire underperforming employees, the business will suffer, and you'll eventually get fired. Just make sure your dismissals are righteous. Does this person really deserve to be fired? I've sat in meetings where upper management had a spreadsheet sorted in ascending order of worker salaries and drew a line on it. We were then told employees with the higher salaries below the line must be dismissed. When it's strictly a numbers game, our ability to understand the individual value of the human being has been lost. That's not the kind of place where I would want to work or stay much longer if I was already working there.

Here are a few final aspects about quitting or being fired. People have a right to work where they want. They may change, sometimes moving from the happy, productive "employee of the year" to becoming a drag on the entire organization. As much as they are negative and miserable, for whatever reason, they remain on the job poisoning the well every day. In this situation, you should have a conversation and convince them that's it's time to move on. There are other workers who become disgruntled after they pitch an idea to their boss which gets rejected. At one of my companies, two guys resigned and started their own business after their idea for a software app was rejected. Ironically, the company they left bought their new company for millions. It would have been cheaper to have financed their idea, but there's always risk attached to a new venture. The good news is after the acquisition the two guys came back to the company and helped us grow even more.

Not everyone who leaves or gets fired should become dead to you. You never know. Some might come back later and be a wonderfully new and improved version of themselves. It happens. Anthony Scaramucci was fired from a financial company, only to come back to that same company after he matured and learned more. My final advice on this topic is to do all you can to keep quitting and firing to a minimum. Terminate an employee only when you must. Most importantly, never burn bridges. That smoke is bad for business.

16. Maintaining Success

If you locate great people, interview them, hire them and train them properly, you will most likely be successful. Of course, it also takes a little good timing and luck, but you already knew that. After you achieve your goals, meet your projections and plan for more success, you cannot take a vacation. You must protect what you've achieved and focus on maintaining it.

I have managed people for more than fifty years and here's my best advice for you. Understand that even though everyone has been created equal under the sun of our planet, people are different. Even when employees form a workplace team, they are not a monolithic group. As much as you want to think of them as one unit, you must be able to mentally separate the individuals when solving problems. It's a careful balance between caring for each employee, but not getting too close and emotionally attached to any individual, which could lead to poor choices. Deploy a well-established, consistent set of values for your company. People feel so much better when they believe things are fair. You must balance the needs and desires of each team member while managing the overall goals and strategies of the collective.

As mentioned earlier, annual reviews are more symbolic and usually part of a mandated company procedure, but working with someone for 240 to 260 days a year demands you know them well. Do they hang art of men climbing mountains in their cubical or do they bring nothing personal into their workspace? You should be able to talk to those who work for you about how they feel, their ideas for doing things better and what will motivate them to work harder and more productively. Yes, I have approved those expensive adjustable "sit or stand" desks for computer workers with bad backs. It was worth it! They worked harder and more efficiently. Constantly monitor the people who want to stay in one place to be consistent worker bees, as well as those who strive to advance or move into management. Always have a certain amount of routine and stability in the workplace without losing the opportunity to add occasional surprises or even outrageous, fun behavior. Make your employees laugh as much as you can because a happy workforce is productive.

I have always believed little events can truly pump up a team, like having people wear costumes on Halloween. Even if there are some who will never dress up, you will see them smiling and laughing at their co-workers. I have also seen unplanned breaks bring freshness to a workday. Even a fire drill, where everyone must stand in the parking lot for twenty minutes, breaks the monotony and brings a different dynamic to the day. While standing outside waiting to get back into the building one day, some of my co-workers came up with a solution for a problem we were grappling with for weeks.

There are harmful distractions and there are productive timeouts to keep people energized. So much of today's work is done while sitting in front of a computer screen. Looking out of the window occasionally not only provides a short pause, but it's healthy to readjust your eyes and physical focus.

Back in the old days at the Apple Computer company, programmers wrote code all day and night. They were given the freedom to hyper-focus on their jobs. Each pod had a refrigerator full of apple juice bottles. Not only was that clever branding, it also provided a true benefit to the workers. Here's a key point. Nothing brings people together better than food. During my first trip to Google's office in lower Manhattan, I noticed a restaurant was available to everyone who worked there and their guests. Where else can you get a free custom omelet to start your day? Do you have something important to share with your team? Take them out to lunch for a meeting and feel the positive energy. Events like "Free-Food-Friday," where the company brings in a caterer for lunch and all managers and employees eat together, bolsters good attitudes and creates a family atmosphere. Some company's budgets are tight, and pennies must be counted every day. So, it may be no soup for their staffs, but there are cost-free ways to keep things positive.

I am drawn to the Employee of the Month pictures on the wall at my favorite grocery store. It's certainly not something that will get them a Wikipedia page, but it's a great gesture. The celebrated workers will feel good, but what happens to the guy who never gets on the wall? Are the awards we give out great for the winners, but a slight for the less productive players? Make sure you have an achievable index for awards. I remember my parents offering us kids $100 if our report cards contained only As. My older sister Donna did it. I was so jealous and wondered how she could have gotten all As. In all my school years I never received a report card with all As, but my kids did many times. Knowing that any of them could get all As, I never offered the deal to my kids. That forced them to find more creative ways to get their hands on my money.

There are things you should never say to someone who works for you. For example, under no circumstances should you compare someone's work with a co-worker in a taunting way. I have heard things like this in the workplace, "I wish you could do that work more quickly like Bob. He rarely makes a mistake." Really? What a terrible thing to say to someone. You should focus only on a person's work, and if you must compare their productivity use a general approach such as "The average car assembler installs 35 bumpers every day, compared to your 28." However, before taking such a step, find out if something is impeding the worker. Maybe the team sending the cars down the line are always late coming back from lunch. There are times when an external event can disrupt a worker's productivity, or it could be that a larger team is driving up the averages you're using for comparison.

Most manufacturing is based on time and productivity. You need to turn out a certain number of widgets during a shift while keeping the quality of work consistently high. If the speed of production lowers the quality of your product, you must evaluate the methods **and** the people doing the work. It's never easy hearing someone tell you the production line has hit a wall. A close investigation might reveal a simple way to maintain productivity and quality. Sometimes a team member knows their productivity is being lowered by actions or inactions of another employee who they like, and they don't want to soil that person's reputation by pointing out their weakness. You must always be vigilant. observant and analytical to uncover the true causes of any problem.

Rewards, bonuses, perks and prizes normally drive people to do amazing work, but not all people are motivated by gold. Some will do quite nicely with acknowledgement and motivation. I am not talking about small gifts, surprises or holiday parties. It's the simple, "If you do that, we will give you this," type of motivation. Some people would be very inspired if the company gave them a company phone, a laptop, extra day off or tickets to a show.

I have wagered some big bucks on broadcast ratings bonuses because I always thought I would do well. When one doesn't make a bonus but has already purchased the boat, this causes panic and unnecessary pressure. As a manager, you've got to keep your eyes open and see if getting or not getting a big payout affects your crew members. Sometimes a person will turn into a monster after winning the big prize.

Some top level managers have the power to award stock options or shares of a company. In our capitalist society this can be a wonderful gift. Typically, front line workers are not eligible for this kind of bonus, which is usually a perk given to top or middle management. Should you be awarded this kind of gratuity, you become privy to company statistics from the annual reports and stockholders' meetings, but remember that you then have a fiduciary responsibility to protect the value of the company. Also, keep in mind that the value of that stock can go down, as I have experienced in a few situations. On the other side of that coin, however, I have seen young people in startup tech businesses quickly become millionaires.

The term attrition is often used in business. It refers to the natural reduction of a company's workforce due to employees dying, retiring or leaving on their own accord for an opportunity at another firm or taking a new job in a totally different field — like the doctor who begins working as a standup comic or the chef who takes a construction job. People change, and some may walk a path veering away from your company. That's fine, but here is the big question. Are you prepared?

If you look at the potential numbers of workers who might retire from your company in the next several years, you'll have a fair idea about when you'll need to replace them. It's not that you want to face the arduous task of replacing legacy employees who know where all the bodies are buried, but sooner or later you will have to find others to replace those "irreplaceable" workers. This is where it gets tricky. If you don't have a plan you can deploy when people leave, the workers who stay behind may get antsy. Most people don't like change, and too many changes may trigger instability and chaos. Companies like FedEx and UPS have been building their teams for years and don't miss a beat when it comes to competing. After all, they aren't like the Post Office which gives all its profits back to Congress each year.

Your company might not be as big as the entities just mentioned, but you share with them the major responsibility of making sure someone is there every morning to make the donuts. If you are not constantly scanning your database for potential worker defections, then you are not doing your job. If you are not doing research on potential new hires, you'd better be training assistants and making sure newer workers are advancing and preparing for a promotion to future changes and challenges.

Here's an exercise to help you. Get a legal pad and make three columns. In the first, list those people who you never want to lose. In the second, catalog those who might be ready to advance. In the third, list workers you suspect may not be around for the long haul or employees you would cut immediately should you be forced to reduce your workforce. Stare at the paper for a few minutes to commit the names and rankings to memory, then shred it. Now you have a mental picture. Find out what those extremely valuable workers need to be happy and spend time motivating them. For the workers ready to advance, make sure you tell them how valuable you think they are or, even better, promote them when you can. Occasionally ask questions like, "What do you think we should have done here?" It's not only planting the seed that you want their input, but how they answer will help you evaluate them for future leadership roles. Have these discussions one on one and never in front of others. It could be your advancing employee will have comments about one or more of their co-workers which they would likely stifle if others are around.

Most people don't openly disagree with their "superiors," and on a completely different note, just who started using that word in the business world? It sounds like something from a prison movie, connotatively and psychologically sending a message that if you are my superior then I must be your inferior. What human being wants to think of themselves as inferior? We use the word "boss" in America and it has some positive connotations. Bruce Springsteen was always referred to by his bandmates, as "the boss." The word is derived from the Dutch *"baas"* which means "master." People have normalized the word, while some will modify it with terms of endearment like "bastard boss," "bitch boss" or perhaps something less printable.

Believe it or not, there are people who love their bosses and look forward to getting up each day and working with them. Aim high here. You can be a great boss without being a hard ass. You're not their "superior," you're simply supervising, guiding, motivating and leading your workers. How you conduct yourself will determine how far your company will go with your team. If you cannot honestly say to your workers, "When I do well, you'll do well," then something is wrong.

People want enough power and responsibility to control a reasonable amount of their own destiny in the workplace. Some employees believe their fate is predetermined. Optimists believe life is better when they have a say about things that affect them. The other side of this equation arises when people feel that no matter what they do or say no one really cares about them. There are some who work hard but are not able to advance in the company. They may lack the skills, the schooling or even the interest to ever be considered for an advanced position. Remember that janitors and receptionists are filling necessary positions and are part of your team. Don't ever make them feel they are simply a cog in the wheel. Remember, without cogs the wheel doesn't turn. Treat these kinds of folks with professional kindness and respect. If the lady who cleans your office doesn't come into work each day, you will be swimming in trash and garbage. All workers have a purpose in the workplace and everyone should always be respected.

This chapter doesn't mention compensation because I want to drill down and focus on that supposed cure-all. It's coming up, right after the break.

17.   Show Me the Money

In the 1996 movie *Jerry Maguire*, Cuba Gooding, Jr. played football player Rod Tidwell and spoke the classic line, **"Show me the money!"** to Tom Cruise in his role as sports agent Jerry Maguire. The cliché was born, and it almost eclipses one other great line from that film, "You had me at hello." Most people like money, while some "love money" and believe their value as a person is based totally on their wealth. The elite judge their prosperity against others to determine their value. Status and wealth go arm and arm down the yellow brick road.

Your employees don't know their value to your company in terms of dollars. A good manager never shares the salary of one employee with another. Only top-level managers should be privy to those numbers. In some organizations the hierarchy has been welded into place by labor unions and company traditions. In the government each job position is assigned a number and a maximum salary for each level of worker. People know that the president's press secretary makes a maximum of $179,000. You probably have no idea how much money the person sitting next to you is making on the job unless they tell you. Comparisons are not healthy and can destroy morale in the workplace. That aside, as a manger you must constantly be asking why one person makes a higher salary than another. Is there justification for two people doing the exact same job having different salaries? Is it seniority? Is it a special skill or training that one has over the other?

In an ideal world, we would focus on individuals and their skill sets, but time, tradition and law are other parts of the equation. Some experts and economists claim the reason women, on average, make less than men in certain fields is because they were late to the game. Well, that excuse is slowly falling out of favor because of many wrongful terminations and lawsuits surrounding wages and equality. If a woman is dissatisfied because her company pays her less than a man in the same position, she might want to consider another job at a different firm or asking her boss for equal pay. Experts agree that in situations of gender pay differentials, for the women it's much like interest being compounded daily. They can never get ahead.

I have a suggestion. Look at your team and determine which women are doing the same jobs as men, then work to make sure they move into the same pay grades. The day of reckoning is coming. If these disparities are disclosed during a lawsuit, you will lose credibility with your workforce. Perhaps you can define rate cards for the various positions in your company, built upon a hierarchy of responsibilities. If a person is named "assistant foreman," give him or her the wage associated with that position. If someone is named "senior developer," then they should get the salary defined for that position regardless of gender, race, religion and so on. A key part of your job is eliminating unfair wages. Your approach should not be draconian; make it flexible and be creative. Maybe additional vacation time can be given to certain people as a bonus. That might motivate some workers, but do check with your HR department before making such an offer. Some states have laws governing how vacation time is dispersed and used.

From the age of Karl Marx through the time of union power to the era of Bernie Madoff, we have constantly struggled to evaluate the worth of individual workers. A professional quarterback might be paid $25 million annually, while Madoff has earned life in prison.

One of the arguments fat cats use to stop minimum wage increases is the dreadful suggestion that making a boss pay you more will lead to your company suffering financially and workers being laid off. While this might be true in some firms and situations, without periodic pay raises workers will eventually feel left out. It can be very traumatizing for a worker to walk into the boss's office and ask for a raise. If an employee must ask you for a pay increase, they are either thinking you forgot about them or you don't believe they are good at what they do. Companies need to be more transparent about raises. If a business cannot afford wage increases, then they should explain where the company is going, why raises are off the table and when they might return. Be careful here. You don't want to eliminate pay hikes when your CEO makes $8 million a year and there are three corporate jets in use by the uppermost executives. In such a case your policy will certainly appear disingenuous.

In some companies, promotions can be viewed in the same way as raises and for the same reason. There may be a limit to the number of people in a job category, and even though an employee has worked hard to move into that job, until someone quits, retires or dies, there will be no further promotions into that position. How do you hold off someone who richly deserves a promotion and can't have it? When an employee's advancement conflicts with the timetable of corporate planning, you may promise but please be clear explaining it might take a while. Never give an employee unreasonable hope if it's not going to happen soon.

In my fifty years in business, or sixty if you count being a newspaper boy, I have made a minimum wage, earned a union salary and, in some years, made tons of money. I always tried to earn a salary that would afford me a comfortable lifestyle. When I was younger I didn't' need much, but after I got married and children came along, more important priorities came to be. After my kids grew, I was able to maintain a good, happy quality of life, but I would be a fool to say that having more money didn't matter to me. I am a full-fledged capitalist and proud of it, but what about the people who work for you?

The Douglas Test, which was covered earlier in this book, can provide insight into the importance a person places on money, but situations also play a role. There is a huge difference between a worker who must pay out tons of money to their sick kid's doctor and the employee who has a serious gambling problem, but each will likely keep asking for a pay raise. It might be better to codify annual reviews and link them to pay raises than making people believe that they can ask for more money whenever the mood hits them. That is no way to run a business.

Where a person lives has a great effect on how much money they make. I know of a company with offices in Fargo, North Dakota and Chicago, Illinois. The people in Chicago made more money than workers having the same job responsibilities in Fargo due to the cost of living difference between the two locations. External forces often affect what a company pays, and it's legal to factor location into wages. A worker in Fargo can request the same wage as her Chicago counterpart, but short of moving to Chicagoland it probably won't get her a higher salary. Healthcare can also vary from state to state due to working conditions, local exemptions and overall policies established at a specific plant. Keep in mind, it's not healthy to have employees think their only chance for upward mobility is to ask for a transfer. They should know how far they can go pay-wise within your company or corporation. I know of at least one state where a law was in place that stated sick days constantly accrued and never went away, yet laws in other states require earned sick days to be reset to zero at the start of each calendar year. If you or one of your staffers want to move to a big city, don't forget to consider state and local taxes. Some cities, like New York, charge you money to work there. Currently, it's 3.876% of your income, and jeez, parking in New York can cost $50 or more a day.

To some workers, sick days and vacations days are like gold in their pockets. You should respect the systems you have in place and make sure everyone is spreading out their vacation days through the year. You want to have enough workers to cover the winter holidays, and a good manager will put policies in place to fairly distribute vacation time during those coveted days. Also, make sure your workers understand that the company wants them to take time off. A manager should never scold an employee for taking vacation time, especially in front of other staff members. You want team members to work with you on projects, not against you. If the deposit for the two-week timeshare in Bermuda is non-refundable, you aren't going to get the Boss of the Year vote after destroying your worker's holiday by making them cancel. Employees need to request time off in advance, of course, and you should work diligently to ensure your deadlines and events align with their desired vacation time. Many companies now use web-based software to track salaries, reviews and vacation time to help smooth this process.

In the old days of professional sports, players were taken advantage of because they wanted to play baseball or football in the big leagues. Over time, the value of the entertainment they provided by playing sports grew. After many lawsuits, strikes and fights, the salaries of professional sports players skyrocketed. When someone's wage jumps from $18,000 to $800,000 to $10 million in a few years, the common man or woman might think they are also worth more. After all, look what those guys get for playing games. One of the strange things that occasionally happens in the pro leagues is a player gets a mega contract, then they feel the pressure to perform and don't do as well.

This brings us to a common debate between labor and management about money. Some managers believe people perform only when they are hungry and trying to prove their value. The myth goes something like this, "Once they get the gold, they don't work as hard." Well, I am here to clear the air on this one. Have you ever wondered why people with billions keep working? Hey, my name isn't Sigmund so I can only wonder why some people work harder to continually prove their greatness while others fall into a slump after landing a dream contract. I think most people simply adjust to how much money they make. If a person overspent when they were making less, they will likely overspend when they are making more. If you have such an employee don't confuse their specific money problems with their desire to be successful. Suggest they see a good accountant.

The best people in any industry are aware enough to know what they should be paid. If you work in a certain field, like banking for example, it's likely that the man or woman running the bank is making millions. If that person is fired, sometimes even for cause, they could get a golden parachute of millions. Let's hope that what you get paid is fair and matches the talent and skill you bring to the job. One of my millionaire friends told me how he approached job offers throughout his life. When a new company discussed salary, he requested a super large figure. Some would laugh at him, but others paid him the inflated number. Hey, he's the millionaire.

Make sure your team gets better every year and that you always push to excel beyond the successes already achieved. No matter how much money a person makes, if they do not receive a raise, even if it's small, they have only one of two thoughts rolling around their head, "*Is it me*" or "*Is the company in trouble?*" The worker doesn't think about a company's profit margin and how it affects their take-home paycheck. They know what they made last year, they know how much they paid for healthcare insurance and they are aware of the cost of living increases they must handle. Their stagnant wage has less buying power each year and if you don't solve the raise challenge, you won't keep great people.

A good manager should be aware of things like a worker who used to go out for lunch every day is now brown bagging it, or the employee who stopped wearing new clothes to work. When a worker's wardrobe becomes as predictable as the old food left in the breakroom refrigerator, they may have slipped into status-quo-land. There's no bounce in their step as they walk into the office each morning.

Remember that a manager can't get too involved in their workers' lives. You are not their shrink, doctor, wife, husband, priest or minister. You are simply their boss. You can often ascertain the happiness of a staffer by judging their facial expressions. Some people are harder to read, but you need to make sure everyone working under you is progressing as people and workers.

The truth about many employees is they do not manage their budgets correctly and end up stretching things too far. At the time this book was written, Americans owed $1 trillion to credit card companies. This is in a country carrying $21 trillion in national debt with no end in sight. While not an excuse for over-spending, it's certainly not a secret reality. But what about the worker, what is he or she worth?

Once I got into a heated exchange with my CFO about an employee we were about to lose to a big New York City tech company. We were 30 miles north of the City and this is what I heard, "There is no way we can compete with those large New York companies." Really? That reason seemed bizarre to me since we were so close to the city and competing for workers in the same candidate pool. The reality of the larger picture confronted by some line managers is unimportant. The local division managers are expected to keep wages from growing. The thinking being it's better to sacrifice a great worker and gain control over fixed costs and inflated budgets. It's better to slow down productivity for a few weeks and spend another $5,000 in recruitment costs, than getting into a bidding war with another company over "one guy." Yes, we've all been there. If a competitor is trying to hire away your great people, and their success in that endeavor escalates your budget, you lose control of your long-term planning. Fact: it's almost impossible to lower a wage. Once you raise a salary it generally stays there or goes higher, although sadly we have seen salary decreases during the global pandemic.

Going back to professional sports players, over the years the leagues have added arbitrators to settle wage disputes. The team brings a bunch of stats, the player states their case for a raise with their own stats, and then the arbitrator decides. It's easy to work toward a compromise because both sides know the numbers of home runs, strike outs and salary. The longer they haggle, the more they establish the worth of those achievements for players who come to arbitration in the future. In many industries it's hard to tell what an individual worker is worth. If the average computer programmer in New York City is paid $90,000, companies will have to step up and pay at least the average salary to hire a good person. As in sports, when a computer programmer is brilliantly productive, he's like a twenty-game winner in baseball.

Over the last twenty years, automation has entered the workplaces of many American industries. Sometimes this is viewed as an improvement, such as self-checkout lanes at the grocery store.

Where ten folks once worked the checkout lanes, now there might be only four, with one worker overseeing the self-checkout.

In the auto industry, a task that required 87 workers in the 1950s might need only 13 today. According to Autoalliance.org, the auto industry provided 9.9 million American jobs at the end of 2019, or about 5.1 percent of private-sector employment. In the late 1980s, the industry had only one million workers. Our nation's population has grown from 226.5 million people in 1980 to 331 million in early 2020, so we need more cars which requires more workers, not fewer. By the way, those workers want to be paid more money. That's why they sometimes go on strike.

The term "union" is a dirty word in most small to medium companies. Should you ever face a situation with a union attempting to organize in your workplace, let me share one vital piece of advice. Don't do anything foolish. Get a labor attorney involved from the very first day. There are many laws on the books, and you don't want to be a target or witness in a lawsuit. Workers want to have a fair shot at making the most money they can. Values and rates change quickly. When the fracking industry took off in North Dakota, miners invaded the state and created mini cities. According to experts, some counties doubled in population. It reminds me of the time when a lot of young guys in my generation went to work on the Alaskan pipeline. The pay was great, and those jobs produced lots of millionaires. The oil and gas rushes in North Dakota were shorter, only six years, and less lucrative because of lower prices for gas and oil. They produced the major supply that lowered the prices.

In a town that is always building, like Atlanta, the prospect is very bright for construction workers. You could even build homes with former President Jimmy Carter at Habitat for Humanity. Quality workers have value in the marketplace. Some talented artisans from Mexico do the lathing, plastering and stuccoing of many homes in the south. It's a backbreaking job that requires a learned skill. There are times worker demand is so great in our country that we cannot fill all the jobs we have. When unemployment rates are low and the stock market is strong, you will need to stay competitive with your industry and similar businesses locally. When demand is high for part-time migrant workers or imported workforces, you might be unable to find qualified workers. That's not your fault but do ask yourself if you are training people for tomorrow. Not every coal miner can learn how to program a computer, but there are many skilled jobs in renewable energy, for example, for those who wants to pursue them.

It's not just the money. You must not only keep people out of poverty but elevate them to better places. Many folks just want to have a roof over their head and food on their table. As one young employee once said to me, "As long as I can have the latest iPhone, I'm happy." Unfortunately, not only are there cost increases for the newest phones, everything else in our capitalist sociality has constant price hikes.

If you don't pay people enough, you cannot be surprised if they are forced to work two or three jobs, or if they resign to take a higher paying position elsewhere. Most wealthy people have no comprehension about the cost of living realities the average person faces, but with a little empathy and a lot of planning you can satisfy great people and get them to stay with your company.

Give your employees a solid 401-K plan, decent healthcare insurance and some love. After all, your workers should be your friends, not your enemies. Sometimes employees become somewhat like family members, and there are some companies where your teammates are more fun to be around than your drunken, bigoted uncle.

18.   Humanity & Productivity

Most of us are motivated to be productive, hard workers, fulfilling the need for purpose in our lives while delivering true benefits to our society. The drive for survival pushes us to get out of bed every morning, arrive at our workplaces and get paid so we can provide our families a safe and nourishing environment. Some folks are moved by ambition, praise and stature in the work tribe. Your job is to find good people like those, vet them intelligently and welcome them into your inner circle. Sounds simple, but you know it's not.

People are not "Spock-like" fixed, emotionless robots. They have moods, they have personal challenges and problems and they aren't as transparent about things that are bothering them as much as you may want. In any American workplace team, there are privacy lines a manager must never cross. Sometimes an employee may want your shoulder to cry on, and while you probably don't relish playing such a role in their life, a good manager understands there are times your business goals might require you to be a sounding board for personal drama. Never neglect empathy in your quest to be successful and make money.

The realization of what can unfold when an employee separates from a company has always amazed me. For example, I have seen two people spend more than 40 hours a week working effectively together for years, but when one of them left the company they never talked again. When I ran a successful radio station in Washington, D.C. my social calendar was always booked, but the moment I was no longer the Program Director those dinners, lunches and get-togethers ceased to be. To those so-called "friends," I was merely an opportunity to them, not a buddy. I understood that intellectually, but I must tell you it was a huge emotional letdown. Rather than remaining disappointed in those people, I grew because of my new insight.

Gossip and leaks can truly hurt a company. This was the motivation for a famous World War II poster that read, LOOSE LIPS SINK SHIPS. This American idiom, means "beware of unguarded talk." During wartime, sharing seemingly innocent information to someone other than a deeply-trusted, personal confidant meant the details could wend their way from one person to another and then another and eventually land on the ears of an actor with the power to undermine our army or navy. As in war, loose lips can become a business problem when people leave your employ. Current members of your team may continue friendships and communication with the departed people, which can lead to problems for the business. For example, little questions about common work acquaintances sometime stimulate more detailed observations and probing. You must make it clear to your team members that discussing co-workers with a former employee is probably okay, but they should never reveal business goals, details and strategies.

It's only human for people who work together to discuss work events and share in-house gossip, but such conversations must never extend to those who no longer work for the company. You should always subtlety remind your people that loose lips **do** sink ships. I would avoid a strong threat like "Don't talk to that guy!" If you have open and trusting relationships with your employees, they may volunteer information about the conversations they've had with people who have left the firm. It's important you simply smile and accept the information rather than sending any facial expression of disapproval. You want the G2 from them. (The military intelligence staff unit in the United States Army is known as G2.)

Understanding and motivating humans at work is a tall order for most people who haven't been trained in psychology, sociology or people management. I entered the business world not schooled in those disciplines, but I've learned a lot from my work experiences and the street. My training was less academic and more common sense and hard knocks. You will experience times when you wonder if you are losing control of the group of people you manage. True leadership is being able to listen long enough to a worker's points, but not letting them submerge into a morass of negativity. You must produce solutions, not only for them, but for the company and, thus, your stability.

I've talked with thousands of people who had nothing good to say about their employer or boss. Why is that? Well, beyond the possibility that their boss is an overlord controlling 40 hours of their life each week, some folks just don't deal well with authority. A rebel on your team might be a productive and hard worker, but you must counsel them to control their poison so it won't infect others on the team. This might be a good time to explore what makes people appreciate a boss and whether that increases their productivity.

Former employees of mine have said that I am crazy, too talkative, frightening, overbearing and some have said, BEST BOSS

EVER! We all have our moments and I admit utter shame about those times I slammed doors, screamed at employees and got too close to some of the people who worked for me. I learned powerful lessons from my many mistakes, and that's why I know the ideas I share can lead you to solid, strong governance.

Some people need to be controlled and confronted, while others seek smiles, hugs and reinforcement. Yeah, I know, watch those hugs, but sometimes they just come naturally. I recall the time when one of my employees lost her father. He had come to America from Europe and had been living at her house for decades. When she finally returned to work after the funeral, we encountered each other in a hallway. I walked up to her and put out my arms and she opened hers and accepted my embrace. She needed a hug at that exact moment. Our relationship was mutually strong and trustful enough to make that happen in an unawkward way. That moment was, and should be, rare in business.

One thing to avoid is attempting to motivate any worker by capricious gifting. It will come back to hurt you should others you manage learn they were not rewarded in the same way. So, if not gifts, what's in your motivational toolbox? Let's open the lid and have a look.

The first tool you have is your face. I know that sounds funny, but it's true. The way you greet and react to people with your facial expressions is a huge part of communication. As we all suffered through the global pandemic, most of us concerned citizens wore masks when shopping or being in situations where social distancing could not be achieved. I had a strange realization early in the pandemic when I saw my next-door neighbor at a store and he didn't know who I was. My mask was obscuring my nose and mouth, blunting recognition and communication. When I smiled inside my mask, no one got the message. I would suggest you use a mirror to check out your reflection. Practice facial movements to communicate various thoughts and feelings. You might like what you see, and this exercise could help you use facial expressions to enhance communications with your workers.

Your mouth and eyes send many subtle messages that convey a broad range of emotions. When you are having a bad day, your face may transmit the stress, conflict or disappointment to those who see you. Is that what you want? My face turns bright red when I get angry. The faces of some people have a natural contour that makes them appear to be always smiling. There was a professional baseball player named Andruw Jones who always appeared to be smiling. He had that built-in look, even after a strike out. Some fans thought he didn't care, but he was an intense competitor. A clown paints a smile on their face to hide emotion. They want to look endlessly happy, but sometimes they just look creepy.

When approaching another, give a bright smile when they say "Hi." If you do, they will probably respond in kind and like you more. If you come across a person wearing a distorted and tense face, you might be able to unarm them with a sincere smile. I know it sounds too simple, but it is. I talk a lot about listening, but all of us are also constantly transmitting. If you give a person an "I just ate a lemon" look when they present an idea they have been working on, you are certainly not going to make them feel good. Always remember that a negative glance from you at an inopportune can kill morale. A simple smile on your face for each of your workers could help them become better employees.

I used to give speeches and conduct seminars all around the world. I remember an occasion when I was presenting research findings in Aruba to a group of broadcasters from Pennsylvania. After years of working on my public speaking approach, I knew the more I looked out at the crowd the better the audience understood my meanings and points. I saw people nod their heads during my presentations, and that encouragement helped me do a better job. When I told a joke, the laughter was instant and infectious. When I smiled after a sentence, I saw that smile mirrored back.

After the presentation, I shook hands with a guy in the front row. He was Ralph Guild, a famous, radio sales executive. During my presentation, I saw Ralph constantly shaking his head in approval. He congratulated me on a good speech and then told me about a trick he used to train newly hired sales reps. He would bring the newbie into a big conference room filled with seasoned sales execs and ask him to give his sales pitch. Just when the guy lost his initial nervousness, the veteran onlookers would shake their heads "No" after each of his major statements. Cruel? Yes, but it was a great test. Many times, a novice presenter would become defensive and keep repeating his point, as if that would change the way they shook their heads. When a newcomer was not at all affected or distracted by the negative feedback in the room, Guild and his crew knew they had found a warrior. Then, they would discuss the fine point of the trick, which was teaching the most important aspect of sales: dealing with rejection. Always remember, faces are powerful.

Another method that should be in your toolbox is the ability to layer a compliment with a suggestion on how to make better whatever is under discussion. Simply smiling and saying something like, "That's really interesting. You might have something there," will get your worker's attention and make them feel good about themself. However, were you to say, "That's great! Did you try it in blue?" not only compliments your team member but suggests the incorporation of a better way. Whatever you do, don't say it like this, "That's not bad, but it would be much better if it was blue. I would make it blue." That would tear a hole in their self-esteem. The key in the best approach is, "...did YOU try it in blue?" You are giving them power over their idea, rather than being a control freak boss.

Another tool you must deploy at times is separating two workers who are arguing about how their opposing ideas can win the day. This is an age-old business drama and it's important not to take sides. You want to invigorate a healthy debate of the pros and cons of each idea in a setting where judgement is low, and analysis is the focus. Hey, everybody wants to be right but, as the leader, you should be nodding your head to reinforce every point discussed. You might bring in someone who has a unique talent of asking Columbo-like questions to get to the real strengths and weakness of the two concepts. It's probably not a good idea to announce an immediate decision. Later, spend time one-on-one with the person whose idea you rejected.

Explain why you made the decision and see if there are parts of their idea that could be incorporated into the final plan. Keep it short and positive. It's not productive to have the person present their idea again but keep them on your radar to see if the situation has a lasting edge that may need your attention.

As you deal with the daily challenges of running a business and handling people, you too will need motivation. I'm amazed when I hear people tell me stories of bosses who never look at them, never ask how they are doing, or worse, what they think the company should do. I have always wanted to communicate with the most powerful person in my company and, for the most part, my career has given me that advantage. If you watch the TV show *Undercover Boss*, you know it's possible the company leader has not met many workers and they might not even know what that person looks like. There will be times when you need to believe in and trust the person at the top. Sadly, there is a lot of cynicism in American business management. Maybe it came about because of TV shows like *The Apprentice* or usually funny *The Office*, but those aren't real. They are terrible examples of American business.

I know a few remarkable owners and bosses who thrived on the dubious process of facilitating inner conflict in the workplace. Maybe they were thinking about a TV show or game dealing with the interactions of people who were pitted against each other. Just know that any survival of the fittest routine will get taxing, especially when you are tasked with maintaining productivity. It's not a game, it's business. You will be wise to apply the old maxim "the shortest distance between two points is a straight line" to help your company make money and be successful. If people or factions are battling it out to see who has the best idea, a possible outcome is the loss of good employees. When the sting of a loss doesn't go away, some people resign. Diverting energy into conflict might produce some interesting and even exciting drama, but does it move the numbers in the right direction?

Some readers may send feedback that internal contests can make things dynamic and keep people on their toes, but when toes are stepped on in a negative way, you must either create a new contest or work to repair injured feelings. Having two individuals or teams compete to solve a problem with a dangled reward for the winner might help them get "skin in the game," but you've got to keep everything positive. Also be watchful of any taunting of the losing team by the winning team. Not cool.

Working with the owner and president of a major broadcasting company who was going to sell his firm and move into the phone business, gave me some insight about human behavior. Before leaving, he wanted to promote someone to his position so that he could hand the company over to the new owner with a strong leader already in place. He divided the properties of the company into two divisions, something that was never done before. He then took his two favorite people and put them into Executive VP positions at the two newly formed divisions. Well, it didn't take long before the different management styles and techniques created confusion and disarray —

one policy for one division, a different one for the other. My position as a consultant was difficult, but it was much worse for the employees.

In the end, only one president survived and after the sale they both left the company. Maybe the owner didn't think one person could handle the entire business, even though he did it himself for years. Maybe his ego wouldn't allow him to see that one person could have done his job. There are already simmering rivalries and future revolutions brewing in any highly charged organization. Why invent conflict when there is no proof it makes humans more productive?

Here's a simple approach. Make sure your workers know you are the boss, but also exhibit an aura of kindness so they see you as someone with enough humanity to make this thing called "work" worth their time, commitment and loyalty. Oh, and never forget to throw some fun into the mix along the way. We learned much about humans' need to work during the global pandemic. People must work not only for money, but also to provide a sense of purpose in life. Forcing people to work in confrontational conditions will not make you a good boss. By explaining your position clearly and strongly, giving logical reason why things must be done in a certain way and listening to employees' questions and comments, you will gain their trust. These are the tools to help in this effort, no matter where you work.

Let's now cap this concept of humanity and productivity. There is one important, large and precise instrument you can use in a surgical way every day to motivate your workers. It's **pride**. You must communicate your belief that **the things your employees do are**

important. Tell them how proud you are of their progress and accomplishments and urge them to feel pride as well. Master that, and you'll be able to motivate your people to do anything.

19. Conclusions & Inclusions

Let's end as we started, with promises. I promised to give you advice to use in your quest to hire great people. By reading, you promised to give my nuggets of wisdom at least a little attention or, better yet, you are ready to integrate some of these ideas into your workflow. But wait, there's more. Every time you hire someone, you make a promise to that person. They applied to your company, or they submitted a resume to your search firm, and now they're sitting in front of you. You asked them to come in for an interview, which is somewhat of a promise to them they have a fair chance of being hired. Having someone interview at your company, even if they had to pay to park for the meeting, places you under no obligation to hire them. They should not expect to automatically get the job, but you've made a small, initial promise. Unless there is some unforeseen problem that takes place, you must interview them. By the way, making an applicant wait in your lobby for any considerable time past the scheduled appointment is not only disrespectful, it's a disregard of a basic human and professional promise.

There are certain realities in business. We can all pity the person who quits their present job to accept a position at another place of employment, only to be laid-off within weeks of getting there. If you don't believe this happens, it does. My brother-in-law moved his family 3,000 miles from the east coast to join a company and take on a new position in California. He was dismissed about a year into his new job. Did I mention he and my sister bought a house? Things eventually turned out quite well for my brother-in-law. He started his own business and became successful, but that change of mind in the company he originally joined didn't make sense. Sometimes there are events churning behind the scenes at the home office that the local and regional people don't know about. There are times when sudden downsizings come without warning. There are situations where the person doing the hiring is fired or resigns before their new employee works their first day. It's not necessarily ethical for a company to dismiss the new hire of a manager who just left, but they might examine the steps that caused the quick cuts.

In the rarified air of the CEO and CFO offices, the term EBITDA is often used. It's an acronym for **E**arnings **B**efore **I**nterest, **T**ax, **D**epreciation and **A**mortization, which is used to judge the performance of a company, or unit within a company, without considering mercurial aspects such as interest on loans, local taxes, depreciation of buildings and equipment or lawsuit payments. All such things could have happened before a new local manager was put in charge, meaning they are completely out of his or her control.

In the grand scheme of business, most corporate offices continually review spreadsheets of budgets and revenue streams. It's their fiduciary responsibility to know which units are making budget, delivering profit or overspending. In this territory, things can get stressed and seemingly unfair.

When an accountant from the home office evaluates numbers on a page, they don't see Dolores in accounting or Pete the maintenance man. They see only the expense of their salaries and benefits. When they are tasked to find the solution to an unprofitable situation, they simply cut numbers without thinking about the real people whose lives will be affected. It's not a bargain with the devil, it's just their job. Of course, those people who I at times affectionately call, bean counters have a very keen understanding of the budgetary realities. They also know they could be cut at any time if they don't prove their worth. In the end, however, management usually goes last, not first. New hires are often scrutinized when a firm needs to make employee cuts because the common wisdom is the least amount of money has been invested in them. That's why you must do your best to hire great people and understand, ahead of time, their path through your firm. If you have any knowledge or suspicion that your new team member could be the victim of an upcoming cutback, don't hire them.

Here's a dicey scenario. Let's say your company is asking you to hire new people who will get lower wages than some of the longer-term employees they will later ask you to fire. I think any boss who assigned you such a task should be fired themselves. In most cases there is no law against this, but it can lead to severe problems for the company. The first and most obvious is employers cannot discriminate against members of protected categories or classes, such as employees over 40 years of age. If an employer disproportionately fires older workers, it's possible they may be found to be engaging in illegal discrimination. It's for this reason that most "culling the herd" business restructuring is usually carried out over a long period of time and often under the table. These laws were put in place to protect workers. Think about a new boss who is a racist and starts replacing minority employees with white workers. You can imagine that discovering and dealing with such a situation would be very costly to the company. You, as a manager with the responsibility of hiring people, should be free of any concerns about the quick changes in upper-level corporate plans. If you have been given the task of replacing a worker who has left, or if you are part of an expansion of the workforce within your company, you should base your decision solely on the capabilities of those you will fire or hire.

There's a thin line between labor and management. As we discussed earlier, you must always maintain a proper emotional and personal distance from your workers. There is the happy day when you have hired them and they start the job, and the wonderful reward of seeing them get traction and grow, but never forget that on another day you may have to discipline them, or worse, fire them. One of the more difficult challenges a manager must face arises when your industry attracts unpredictable and crazy people who are extremely talented performers. The radio industry is a great example because it is filled with fanatical but gifted on-air performers. Just because they are twisted or extreme doesn't mean they can't be great communicators on the radio. There was a day when I told a DJ that his on-air work sounded down, almost depressing. He immediately opened his briefcase, pulled out a prescription medicine bottle, opened it and popped two pills. Within minutes he was his happy, effervescent self again. I didn't ask what he was taking. That would be against the law.

You want people to believe and say you are a great boss, but that compliment should never be associated with this additional qualifier, "He lets us do whatever we want!" People cheat at work more often than you might think, like having someone else punch you in at the time clock. Security cameras have ended that practice but there are other things in the workplace to which some people might feel entitled. I once caught a worker in the supply closet loading up a shopping bag with toilet paper. Why would a person do that? My company gives its employees free sodas and coffee, so why steal from the hand that feeds? One of your major responsibilities is keeping team spirit up without having anyone believe they deserve special privileges or gifts and while not creating an environment that feels like a prison. It's a balancing act, but one you can learn.

Your company should be posting its rules and regulations in a common area, such as the breakroom. Some are state mandated notices, while others are released by the US Department of Labor or other federal agencies. They disclose minimum wages, rules about the age of workers and other such legalities. You should urge your workers to read them. They might find it comforting to know someone cares about them. I am certain nothing they will read there will ever damage your company. You should also read and follow those directives since you always need to be on the right side of the law.

It's time for every employer to broaden their frame of reference because when unemployment decreases, the demand for good workers increases. A constant goal should be thinking ahead to your next need to hire. Strive to increase the number of contacts you can use for referrals and develop and maintain a list of places to find potential hires. If your candidate pool is not growing, you will be unable to find the great candidates when the need arises. Study your competitors and try to determine where they found their best employees. If they are tapping a university for top graduates, you need to spend time on that campus to make your company better known.

We talked about temperaments of people and how you cannot use a single filter for every employee or potential hire. People are different and they always grow and change. Life would be boring if the person you hire today is the same five or ten years from now, but as they progress make sure the company moves with them. If a worker wants a better position and goes to night school to learn a new aspect of their job or industry, see if your company can tap into that enthusiasm and drive. One excellent way of doing this would be partially or completely funding their tuition. After all, your firm is benefitting from their initiative. If that idea makes you nervous, you could ask your worker to sign an agreement that after you pay for the additional learning, they will stay at your company for a defined length of time.

Always be honest with those you manage. If it will be impossible for a worker to move to a different division or job in the company once they compete additional training or education, let them know that up front. You never want to be negative, but if your company is a window factory and your worker is attending masonry classes, that's probably not the right path for them to grow in your business. Make sure they understand global planning and work assignments, especially if it's out of your hands. You must always manage the workers' expectations.

On the other side of things, I have seen software coders study and learn on their own to enhance their development team and its efforts. It takes a self-starting personality and high ambition to invest time, energy and possibly dollars in learning new skills, and wonderful workers like this need your support. Hard workers should be valued and rewarded.

I hope that you try out the Douglas Test on one of your next applicants. You might find it an easy way to understand various personality aspects of the candidate without any illegal probing or expensive testing. It's just one idea from this book that could make a huge difference in your success.

If you take anything away from my writing, please understand and remember how important the first day on the job is for any employee. Recall the night before each of your new jobs and how you laid out the clothing you were going to wear and the excitement you felt just thinking about walking into your new workplace the next day. It's important to immediately make your new hire feel welcome at their new place of employment. Some companies have a ritual of taking a newbie around to every desk and office, introducing them to their new co-workers. If you're not doing this, you should be. It's a short, easy effort that will make your fresh hire feel welcomed and important. By the way, there is also a security aspect to this. It allows company employees to see the new face and know that person belongs.

One of my friends told me about this experience. On his very first day on a new job his boss asked him, "So what do you want to do?" My friend replied with a short rundown of his new job description. The boss replied, "No, that's not what I mean. How would you like to grow and advance here?" My friend more or less said he would eventually like to have the job of his new boss, who replied "We'll do all we can to make that happen," and just a few short years later, it did. My friend claimed this was the highlight of his career because he saw evidence that his new company wanted to help him grow. Your word should be your bond, and you must always follow through on offers or promises. It's a key component in the success of those who manage people.

With all the skullduggery and theft that takes place in workplaces today, it's good for every employee to know who works there and who doesn't, especially if your firm doesn't employ picture identification badges. It's probably a good idea to figure out how to develop a security plan to keep your people safe.

Training is especially important and necessary to the future success of each new hire. We have pointed out how everyone learns differently. Some learn by reading, some learn by watching and some learn by experimenting. I would not recommend the third technique if you are a hospital, airline company or nuclear power plant, but you must determine how each of your team members learn best and develop training procedures tailored accordingly. My time in the software business made it apparent that certain people were great teachers and "go to" resources when others were stumped while learning or working. Should such a person under your employ complain about being taken away from their work, you need to get in there and compliment the teacher for doing such a great job and encourage the participation.

Here is a tip rarely discussed in businesses today. Have your training programs been evaluated? You might want to employ an outside firm to assess your training. Are you cutting corners? Are your materials up to date? You most likely are not objective enough to critique your own training content and methods. I remember a trainee coming to me with a question after reading the training manual. He pointed to a paragraph in the book and asked if it conflicted with another part of the material. I asked him how his trainer answered the question. He answered, "Oh, he said that wasn't valid anymore." So, there's a perfect example of why everything needs to be reviewed regularly. You never want to be teaching incorrect or outdated procedures. Yes, your training content and methods must be continuously evaluated and updated, just like everything else you do at your company.

Managers can be victims of locked budgets and constraints that aren't fair or effective. You may have a chance to hire a great person away from a competitor, but your budget says, "THAT IS THE NUMBER, DEAL WITH IT." Obviously, you wouldn't say that to a prospective employee. As much as you think a potential hire will understand your budget will not permit a larger salary, disclosing that will automatically and rightfully make them think your company isn't as competitive as the one they would be leaving. It could be they will stay where they are and wait for you to become open to their needs. I also have interviewed some cunning negotiators and given them a figure, which they took back to their present employer to renegotiate their pay. Perhaps their employer has a "right to match" clause in the employment contract, which is quite typical. To avoid being played, you should vet every potential hire before making an offer. Also, don't be naïve. Some company contracts stipulate an offer sheet must be seen before they salary-match, so don't let it get that far.

We talked about the safety and protection of your employees. Applicants rarely ask about such things during an interview because they assume your business operates legally and properly. Those beliefs are good and you don't need to be defensive or overly sales-pitchy on the legal and safety records of your company. It's good to make sure any questions they ask on the subjects are answered honestly and completely. If someone, especially a woman, is going to be working a late shift and she asks about the building security, you should be armed with the facts. I once worked in a building that was robbed several times. Imagine how disturbing it was to find out that the locked/pass-keyed door to the parking lot was duct-taped open after hours because a dentist on the second floor scheduled night appointments. People notice such things and not all of them are honest.

As a manager, you must make sure your workers are protected from those outside and those inside. If an employee complains to you about being harassed, you are obligated to report it, even if it's not your department or division. You could be called to testify in a court case after an employee confides in you. We have seen what has happened in many of the #MeToo cases, so never keep your mouth shut. It's not just for the sake of that one person or group of people who are involved, it's for the overall security of your company.

In a sense, each of your employees is a public relations agent for your business. They form a walking, talking advertising campaign. It's imperative that you treat your workers in an honest, positive and motivational manner. People talk among themselves outside of work. Over cocktails or pizza they describe their jobs. For years, people wrote about Bain Capital, an investment company that Mitt Romney started in Boston. For all the bad PR that company received, when they were evaluated by objective, outside firms, their employees rated their relationships with Bain very positively. Yes, I hear you. When employees get million-dollar bonuses they should be happy, but that's the depth of their business. Bain makes tons of money.

Motivated and positive workers are important for all companies, be it the corner grocery store or a multi-national financial institution. There are two large grocery store chains where I live in Florida and I notice a difference between them. One has happy, smiling workers dressed in bright colors. Managers at the other store seem to hire people who aren't necessarily excited about being in that business.

In some industries, turnover leads to a more energetic workforce. People sometimes develop a negative attitude when they hold the same job for too long. Maybe an employee sees the recruitment and training procedures at another company as better than what they have at your firm. Perhaps the benefits they offer and the way they treat their employees are more appealing. It could be your worker feels another company's employees are included in decisions and have more control of their own destinies. Then again, the other firm could simply be viewed as a cooler place to work. When your workers are out in the world, what do they reveal about your company? Will they say you treat your workers well or will they talk about a bad boss, substandard working conditions or lack of respect? You can make a difference by being a fair and open but always firm manager who plays by the rules.

You need to keep your workers fired up, and to do that you must also be fired up. If yours is a larger company, there will be times requiring you to be a salesperson, and other times when you will have to admit that the boneheads in the home office messed up. You will most likely find yourself balancing those two concepts. You are a store, a unit, a family or a special division, while also being part of a greater, more important entity, the owner of the business. That owner, be it a corporation, one or more individuals or a group of shareholders in a publicly traded company can be perceived as either overlord or friend. There is an approach to this that some say is treasonous, but it is a concept that's used. Some crafty managers set up the main hub office as the enemy. They say things like, "It's us against the world, guys!" meaning that we need to do what we have to do and not moan about how bad our owners are. It's the old "our only security is success" mantra. This can work for your employees, but the home office must never find out.

Firings at companies don't have to become a raging crisis or a downer for the workers who get to stay. Simply put, you must provide your workers a believable explanation for the separation of a co-worker. You can't trump up a charge, like, "Oh, no one liked him, anyway." That would make any employee shake in their boots, especially if the person who was just fired was highly liked by the team. On the other hand, there are some legal situations in which you cannot reveal the reason why a person was fired. This one is easy. Put on a serious face and simply say, "It's a legal matter and I can't talk about it." You are telling the truth and most people will understand the departing worker must have done something extremely bad. If a lawsuit is pending, say nothing. In such a case it's okay to say, "No comment" to your people and just walk away. There might be resulting gossip, but you must end or minimize any damage to your company and yourself. If you have been resourceful and your files contain memos documenting the transgressions of a fired person, perhaps with a "three-strikes and you're out" red-line, you might use their departure as a teaching moment. I once told the most active gossiper at my firm that I fired a person because they came late to work too many times. For at least the next six months, all my people came to work on time. Amazing!

Remember the following in your quest to maintain success. Just like you shouldn't fix something that isn't broken, the same can be said for hiring procedures. If you have had success with hiring great people, then keep doing it the same way. While you concentrate on productivity, profits and positive energy, you also are dealing with people. They don't look the same, they don't talk the same and they are all different in so many ways. What is the best advice for maintaining your success?

I would start with flexibility and listening. Be open to expanding and contracting your teams. It's all about the variables of economic flows and the needs of your company. As much as you would like to always build and get bigger, sometimes you may be ordered to get rid of redundancies or introduce cost saving innovations. The garbage truck in my neighborhood used to have three guys, now it has only one. Nowadays a big arm lifts and empties a specially designed dumpster into the truck, and this automation has decreased the workforce. Hopefully, the guys who were laid off can find other jobs, but nothing stays the same. I had to argue to buy the first computer at my workplace some forty years ago. Today, no one would ever think of starting a business without one or more.

Listening carefully to what your workers say they need to do a better job is paramount. Don't wait for them to tell you. Ask them what you can do to make them better at their jobs. You will probably get some great, thought-provoking answers. Listen to the drumbeat within the company and the team. Don't be so isolated that you stay in your office all day and never walk around. One of my co-workers used to make fun of my boss when he canvassed the entire office first thing each morning and just before he left every night. My co-worker joked, "Oh, there goes the boss with his bed check," but the boss was right. When you walk around, you hear and observe things. Yes, there are many suck ups who will take the time to advance their own careers when they chat with the boss, but a good boss sees right through that kind of BS.

How do you know when you've hired the right person? Look for signs such as immediate acceptance by your team. See who they sit with during lunch. Are they engaging with the other workers or do they isolate themselves? Look at their work. Are they being productive and constructive? Tap into their curiosity to learn if they may have a suggestion about a better way to do their tasks. Most importantly, are they happy? If they don't seem happy within the first sixty days, then you hired either the wrong person or a manic depressive.

Your current workers will be impressed when you bring a great person onboard. A work environment gets pumped up when fresh blood comes into the company. In a sense, it challenges the workers who have been there a long time. Sure, attitudes might flare up and there might even be some gentle ribbing of the new guy or gal, but that should pass rather quickly once the newbie begins to show their chops. The maxim that "one rotten apple spoils the whole barrel" is true, and it's your job to make sure that any negative forces are kept at bay until the new hire gets their balance. As a good manager, you should be aware and getting rid of rotten apples. When you hire someone, you don't necessarily have to warn them about the bad one in the barrel, but you might want to send the newbie a message that certain people are more "negative judgmental" than harmful.

It's important to respect peoples' time. I have seen company presidents conduct two-hour meetings filled with tales of their last 18 holes or doing a lame standup routine. Stop it! Just as you would resent someone taking up your time with things having no relevance to the tasks at hand, you should think about your team members when planning and conducting your meetings. You don't want them to be late, so it's imperative that you not arrive late to your own meetings. Be there on time and begin your organized agenda promptly. It's great for your ego to know you are the boss of people but leave that ego at the front door when you come into work each morning. Confidence is fine and required in today's world of business, but don't make people feel inferior or oppressed. You'll get the most out of your staff when you convince them you care equally about their work and each of them as individuals. You cannot give them everything they desire, but you must recognize that most people want to make a difference and that they are people, not machines.

I have worked in large companies with hundreds of local employees and thousands of workers spread across the globe and I have worked in small businesses with less than a dozen people. What I enjoyed most about those widely different experiences were the people. When we downsized our consulting firm and began working out of our homes, the joy of having no commute was felt immediately. Then, something else crept in. Loneliness. Yes, I will confess that as much as I think and say I enjoy working alone; I need people. The challenge most firms are going through right now is deciding who should work from home and who needs to be in the factory, plant or office. The global pandemic in 2020 changed the way we do business and the long-term effects will challenge us forever. The future of the brick building office might be at risk, but the work of some businesses cannot be done from home.

At one of my companies we lost a great salesperson who had a horrible commute and failed at convincing the management that working from home would be more productive for her. There is an outdated management notion that if you can't see a person, they are probably screwing off. After an exhausting argument with her boss, which she lost, she finally resigned and went to work for a competitor that permitted a work-from-home arrangement. Here's the irony of this story. Within six months, the company she left decided that working from home was okay. Shoddy logic is never a good way to keep great people.

A necessary management skill is admitting when you have made a mistake. I have hired some bad guys and eventually realized it was all my fault. There were times when I rushed into a decision and didn't look at a larger field. On other occasions I was lured into hiring someone who had a glowing referral from a former boss, but they failed to live up to the hype. There will probably be an occasion when you will hire someone with negative baggage, but sooner or later you will have to let them go. I am reminded of the movie *500 Days of Summer*, in which Tom falls in love with a girl named Summer. Spoiler alert: At the end of the movie you realize that Summer was giving Tom all the signs that she wasn't as much in love with him as he was with her. We all fall in love with our hires and we want to be right every single time, but one hundred percent just isn't possible.

If you hire a person who is so in debt that they steal from the business to make ends meet, that difficult situation must be handled immediately. Let's say another of your workers has suffered from kleptomania their entire life. If they get arrested for shoplifting, you have a decision to make. The first person in this comparison must be fired straightaway. The circumstances regarding the second person's arrest will help you make your decision. Is the apprehension public knowledge? Will it make your company look bad? Will the worker end up stealing from work? Think it through carefully before deciding, and remember it's always good business to help an employee get treatment for any medically related problem such as mental illness, drug addiction or alcoholism.

Sometimes we hire a perfectly normal, healthy human who ends up becoming a workplace problem in a way that never could have been predicted, like a new male hire's inability to work with women. Ouch! Perhaps it's a guy who has always been a great pitcher but throws out his arm on the first day of practice. It could be the new worker who lied about having experience with a procedure or certain piece of equipment. Do you spend extra time or money training him or her, or should you fire them at once? My advice? Cut your losses quickly. Never keep a liar around. Desperate people do desperate deeds, and when your career and the success of your company depend on every person performing well, keep your eyes open and act quickly and decisively if you have made a mistake.

I always objected to any company that constantly urged employees to support their Political Action Committee (PAC) in

Washington. Clearly, large companies feel a need to shape legislation on Capitol Hill to favor their business objectives, but there is a major flaw in the idea of involving its employees. A company cannot use its own cash to fund a candidate, but they urge employees to help their cause. Since the Supreme Court ruling called Citizens United, companies can legally require workers to participate in politics and fire them if they refuse. This form of employer political coercion will be challenged in the courts and some state laws have stepped up to prevent this activity. The UCLA Law Review covered the Oregon Worker Freedom Act, which prohibits terminating employees for refusing to attend mandatory political, labor, or religious meetings held by their employers. The political plans of a company's lobbyists cannot possibly reflect values of everyone working for the company. Asking employees to contribute to a PAC infers that you don't belong in the firm if you do not support the corporate political policies. It's more dividing than uniting. No business in America has the right to legislate the political or charitable actions of their workers.

Always be alert for your next superstar; they are out there. Hone your skills as an interviewer and be mindful of due diligence. Get to know as much as you can about a person before interviewing them. Let them talk while you listen carefully and be observant to learn who they truly are. Find out what they think about the jobs they've had in the past. See if you can determine how important work is to them. Having someone who wants to work and enjoys their job is far better than hiring someone who is interested only in the paycheck. Every person is an individual and should be treated as such. Don't put everyone in the same box you want them to think outside of. Above all else, always be honest. If you don't know an answer, tell them you will get back to them. Never make a promise you cannot keep. Most importantly, always follow the law because doing so is good business.

Happy hunting, my friend. Find that great person and hire them, train them and treat them the same way you want to be treated. They will do well, and you will do well. In the end, may we all get a greater reward with each new challenge we face.

Thank You Very Much

This book began as a pet project to distill into words the business principals I developed, used and believed in for years. I was halfway into my writing when the COVID-19 global pandemic broke out. It changed the approach of this book. Now more than ever, we need to bring great people back to our workforces and expand our economy to the level we know it can be. Thank you for buying this book. I hope it will inspire you to hire great people and make your business better.

I extend my next thank you to Kenny Lee Karpinski, who has been editing my words and listening to my jokes for more than fifty years. We were classmates in college, and later co-workers in both the radio and software businesses. Without his editing, rearranging and motivating, this book would be less than it is. I must also give a shoutout to my 20-year partner, Roxy Myzal for editing and arguing with me. She always makes great points.

You do judge a book by its cover, and the one wrapped around these pages is fabulous. The talented Ginger Sinton fashioned this stunning book cover. Thanks to Ginger for her creation and hard work.

I have a depth of knowledge about people and business because of the wonderful bosses and company leaders I have worked for and with. I thank Charles R. Reinecker, who was my first boss when I delivered newspapers as a kid in the sixties. He was a great motivator and always treated me fairly.

Thank You Very Much

I had quite a few manual labor jobs when I was in college. I learned how to paint, clean hotel rooms and move 15-ton rolls of strip steel onto a railroad car. Working in a steel mill instilled many rules and regulations related to keeping people alive and gave me a deep respect for safety in the workplace.

In the broadcasting business I met some of the best managers and, sorry to say, some of the worst. This was a major reason why I became a radio consultant. That career allowed me to help many stations at once. My boss at the consulting firm was its founder, Kent Burkhart. He was much more than a boss, and eventually became my father-in-law. Kent enriched not only my business sense but also my interactions with people. I thank him for opening my eyes to the mission and helping me become more productive. I will never forget his always honest and direct evaluations of my work.

Then there's Andrew Economos. I consulted his software company for years before he brought me on as a full-time employee. Andrew gave me the opportunity to travel and work with some of his 14,000 client radio stations worldwide. Andrew instilled in me the viewpoint that any setback eventually shall pass. When we got knocked down, we got right back up and kept going. We hired creative, talented software engineers and managed those geniuses. I learned how to motivate their visions without breaking the bank.

And finally, I thank Charles and Betty Douglas. My parents gave me a solid moral grounding that wasn't focused on churches and religion, but rather on the golden rule and how to treat people. I miss them and love them, forever.

Books that influenced this work

How to Hire, Train & Keep the Best Employees for Your Small Business: With Companion CD-ROM Paperback by Dianna Podmoroff – January 12, 2005 — Atlantic Publishing Group Inc.

How to Hire the Best: The Contractor's Ultimate Guide to Attracting Top Performing Employees by Sabrina Starling — October 24, 2019 — Amazon.com Services LLC.

Recruit Rockstars: The 10 Step Playbook to Find the Winners and Ignite Your Business — by Jeff Hyman — November 28, 2017 —Lioncrest Publishing.

The 22 Immutable Laws of Marketing: Violate Them at Your Own Risk! By Al Ries & Jack Trout — April 27, 1994 — HarperBusiness.

The One Minute Manager by Kenneth Blanchard Ph.D. & Spencer Johnson M.D. — September 1, 2001 — Simon & Schuster & Nightingale-Conant.

From the Ground Up: A Journey to Reimagine the Promise of America by Howard Schultz — January 28, 2019 — Random House.

Kochland: The Secret History of Koch Industries and Corporate Power in America by Christopher Leonard — August 13, 2019 — Simon & Schuster.

OTHER BOOKS BY DWIGHT C. DOUGLAS

If God Could Talk: The Diary of a TV Journalist

A Cable television talk show host is approached by a friend who offers a guest for his show who has never been on TV before. The Diary of a TV Journalist is the story about the host of the show and his executive producer vetting the guest and attempting to determine... If God Could Talk. Available at Amazon.com, GoodReads.com, Barnesandnoble.com

Donald Trump: Repeal, Replace, Impeach

These diatribes of a delusional blogger offer a day by day overview of the 45th President's first two-hundred days in office. Follow Donald Trump through the tough times on his way to impeachment. Available at Amazon.com, GoodReads.com, Barnesandnoble.com

If God Could Cry: The True Meaning of Mercy

The famous cable TV talk show host, Jonas Bronck, leaves New York on a quest to find truth. He finds himself in the middle of terror and personal torment for the sake of journalism. He asks, If God Could Cry, would he be crying for us or with us?

Gold, God, Guns & Goofballs: A Collection of Essays on America

This collection of short articles explores the notion of the corporate state of Gold, scrutinizes the meaning of God in our society, questions our unhealthy need for Guns and lays out the damage that the Goofballs in power have wrought in this great nation.

Made in the USA
Columbia, SC
03 September 2021